The Universal Form

The Universal Form

A Three-Minute Routine for
Transforming Stress into
Power and Peace

by Lawrence Tan

Weatherhill
New York & Tokyo

First edition, 1998

Tan, Lawrence
    The universal form: a
three-minute routine for
transforming stress into power
and peace / by Lawrence Tan.
-- 1st ed.
    p.   cm.
    ISBN 0-8348-0454-9
1. Peace of mind.
2. Centering (Psychology)
3. Body-mind centering.
4. Meditation–Therapeutic
use. 5. Exercise therapy.
6. Stress (Psychology) I. Title.
BF637.P3T36 1998
613.7--dc21   98-36589
                   CIP

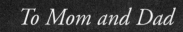
To Mom and Dad

Contents

Foreword

To alleviate the stress and conflict caused by our frantic quest for ever higher standards of living, people today are turning more frequently to spiritual paths for self-discovery and inner peace. The wisdom of the ages suggests that the simplest and most ordinary path to enlightenment may in fact be the most profound and mysterious. Indeed, Hui Neng, the sixth patriarch of Zen Buddhism, said that the true way of the Buddha is found in the smallest details of everyday life. The aim of this unique way is inner peace—freedom from the vexations of daily living and release from the suffering of the human condition; in today's terminology, this aim might be described as a genuinely enhanced quality of life through discovery of inner spiritual riches that transcend the material world. To attain these goals, Zen prescribed the practice of both sitting meditation and Kung Fu exercises, as developed at China's Shaolin Temple some 1500 years ago.

Lawrence Tan here introduces the Universal Form, a short and simple moving meditation exercise to help us relax and focus. Although it is a modern creation, it is evident from its theory and movements that this exercise can be traced to the Zen meditation and Kung Fu exercises practiced over the ages by the warrior monks of Shaolin Temple. By combining the action of the martial arts with the contemplative aspects of Zen, thus synchronizing mind and body, this exercise can bring clarity to the mind, relaxation to the body, and tranquillity to the spirit.

Mr. Tan also introduces Tri-Harmony, his secular philosophy of health and wellness. As with his Universal Form, the influence of traditional Chinese thought is clearly apparent. The fundamental principle of Tri-Harmony is an updated interpretation of the traditional notion of the three forces in life—Heaven, Earth, and Humanity. According to the author, both the wellness principles of Tri-Harmony and his Universal Form are "old wine in new bottles" that can be readily adapted to our modern lifestyles, both to help us cope with stress and to cultivate inner peace.

Master Shi Guo Lin
34th Generation Shaolin Monk
Appointed Overseas Ambassador by Venerable
Shi Yong Xin, Abbot of Shaolin Temple

Preface and Acknowledgments

During my thirty-five years as a martial artist, I have taught many people to find peace by developing the power to defend themselves in violent encounters. However, I came to realize that the chance of a person being attacked on the streets is relatively small compared to the guaranteed assault of everyday stress.

And no wonder, for stress is our universal enemy. With the accelerating rate of change, successive global economic, political, and environmental crises, not to mention the hectic pressures in our professional and personal lives, it sometimes seems that while the cost of living has gone up, our chances of enjoying life have gone down. Is there a way for us to defend and empower ourselves against stress?

The ancient Chinese warrior monks of the Shaolin Temple trained themselves in a physical, psychological, and spiritual self-discipline that embraced both Kung Fu, a way of action, and Zen, a way of contemplation. Power and inner peace: Aren't these really what we all need to defend against the stressful battles of daily living? Power, the goal of the warrior's training, is the capacity to decisively assert ourselves to overcome adversity and resolve conflict, whether related to events or people. And tranquillity, the goal of the monk, is the ability to quietly contemplate and find harmony in life in spite of adversity and chaos. Therefore the Shaolin warrior monk's discipline becomes a metaphor for our own personal quest for harmony in the stressful chaos of modern living.

The purpose of this book is teach the Universal Form, a practical "how to" exercise to defend against stress. It is a unique method because the same exercise can be performed in different ways to achieve different benefits, for example, to energize or to relax, to increase strength or to improve flexibility.

Another goal is to introduce the Tri-Harmony philosophy of health, a system rooted in Chinese traditional thought that seeks the cultivation of the whole human being. Tri-Harmony, a process of unifying the mind, body and spirit, is a holistic way of well-being for the third millennium.

What characterizes the Tri-Harmony teachings are Tri-Harmony principles of wellness underlying the physical exercises. For what the Universal Form is to the body, Tri-Harmony principles are to the mind. Vital ideas on health, like centering and unified awareness, so essential for healthy living, are expressed through these holistic principles.

These potent tools for achieving self-awareness and personal wellness, are formulated according to the central Tri-Harmony principle of Three-In-One (aligning three separate forces into a unified force to maximize power). On the practical level, an understanding of these basic Tri-Harmony principles will help you cultivate a holistic attitude for day-to-day living as well as provide deeper appreciation of the multi-dimensional aspects derived from Universal Form practice.

I created the Universal Form, a moving meditation exercise, by adapting principles and techniques of Shaolin tradition to meet the demands of our fast-paced lifestyles. As with Tai Chi or yoga, you can energize or relax, calm and focus your mind, improve your posture, and enhance daily performance. However, the Universal Form is easier to learn. Most important, it is a practical method to "get it together" any time and any place in just three minutes!

THE TRI-HARMONY SYMBOL, a circle in the center of an equilateral triangle, represents an intuitively aware individual striving for health and well-being through the conscious balancing of mind, body, and spirit.

Although this may sound too good to be true, the benefits of this unique exercise can be attested to by many. It works. But it must be learned properly and must be practiced regularly before it can be done naturally and spontaneously. In the beginning, be patient and practice. In time, you will experience the rewards of the Universal Form as you transform your stress to power and peace. Remember the secret: Doing it *is* it!

This book evolved piecemeal over a decade. During that time many special people have graciously contributed their talents to help turn my fragmented vision into reality. In no particular order, I'd like to thank: Stanley Lee for his diagrams; Jefferson Miles for drawings of the Universal Form postures; Kuling Choy Siegel for the waterfall photos; Cheung Ching Ming for his photos of Universal Form poses; Marvin Bookman for the "master's sword" and Universal Form position photos; Joe Lau for the hand-position photos; Lawrence Di Marzio for the dedication-page photo; Wei Ng for the cover photo: Fleeta Choy Siegel, Christopher Cave, Charlie Bracey, and Rosa Pineda for their computer graphics contributions; Francine Tint for the background painting; Rex Hughes for modeling the Universal Form drawings; Wu Mei Ling for her Wu Shu poses; Lu Chin Chung for his calligraphy; Tom Murphy, Christine Choy, Sandy Ng, Melinda Liu, Mary Claude Foster, and Herbert Berger for reading the manuscript; and Gina Griffin, Jeffrey Callender, and Kimberly Jarden for their computer skills. Special thanks to Dr. Phillip Shinnick, Dr. Celia Blumenthal, and Master Shi Guo Lin for their kind testimonials and support, and to Hagen Christian Volkers, Si-fu Jesse "Two Owls" Teasely, and his students. Finally, I'd like to thank the staff at Weatherhill, especially its editorial director, Ray Furse, and its talented book designer, Mariana Canelo.

To these and all others who I have not mentioned, a deep bow of gratitude, appreciation, and affection.

Lawrence Tan

Introduction

Harmony in Chaos

On the verge of the year 2000, we live in chaos. Our traditional world view is collapsing before our eyes and a new unknown order is dramatically emerging. There is escalating conflict, confusion, and crisis.

Everywhere chaos is evident: globally, with our technological excesses, we are destroying the planet's intricate ecological balance; internationally, with the restructuring of political and economic power, we continue to face the twin threats of war and economic disaster; domestically, there are the growing problems of terrorism, poverty, urban crime, AIDS, drugs and the homeless.

Perhaps nowhere is chaos more apparent than in what we directly experience in our personal lives. For even the security of normalcy, as we once knew it, no longer exists. Gender roles, family relationships, sexual standards, career choices, education, and other conventional values are being reassessed. The very meaning of relationships and our basic responsibility to ourselves, to others, and to the world is confusing.

Clearly our modern lifestyle is characterized by accelerating change, recurring crises, and overwhelming confusion. All this is synonymous with stress. With the growing awareness of the relationship between stress and health, it is no wonder, then, that seeking a healthier life today includes battling stress.

In order to maintain health and foster well-being, we are compelled to ask: Is it possible to achieve personal harmony amidst such chaos? Is there any way to control the stresses of daily living? Can we transform our personal battles of life into a joyous dance? Perhaps we would do well to learn some valuable wisdom and techniques from the ancient martial arts masters who elevated the art of survival into a way of life.

Have you ever witnessed a martial arts master surrounded by a group of attackers? In a flash, the intended victim transforms into the victor. Despite the onslaught of fierce opponents, the master merges with the attacking forces and defends himself, displaying superb physical technique and psychological skill. This is harmony in chaos.

Like the tranquil center of a violent hurricane, the master expresses clarity of thought, emotional calm, and decisive action. Aren't these the same qualities that we could rely on in confronting the chaos of modern living? Wouldn't we enhance our lives if we could think more clearly and act decisively and calmly during a personal crisis or amidst the routine conflicts we encounter at work or at home? The secret key to responding serenely, gracefully, and efficiently to violence is the ability to achieve a state of inner harmony. For harmony there must be the unification of our whole being—mental, physical, and spiritual. Personal harmony, therefore, is fundamentally a state of high-level health and well-being.

What are Forms?

Ancient Chinese martial arts masters developed a unique method of cultivating health and harmony through the practice of forms, dance-like sequences of body postures consisting of specific stances and hand positions. Unlike most dance, however, forms are moving meditation exercises, very similar, but not identical, to Hindu yoga. These specialized exercises incorporate elements now understood by researchers to relate to the modern sciences of biomechanics, psychology, physiology, and metaphysics.

Although many martial artists practice forms, which vary from style to style, few realize the profound implications of the hidden layers of meaning inherent in the movements. To be sure, many do eagerly seek to find the secret combat techniques or subtle strategies found in forms that are alluded to by the masters and martial tales. Yet forms are intricate riddles that go beyond the science of destruction.

Actually, although the pre-arranged sequence of postures clearly have fighting applications, the forms were initially conceived by Buddhist monks and Taoist priests to be graceful moving meditation exercises for cultivating health and superior mental and physical fitness. Thus, the original intent was for self-development; only later did the emphasis shift to self-defense.

A form is much more than a physical exercise; it is a book of knowledge. Ideas and information on health, fitness, healing, self-defense, spiritual awakening, and philosophy are expressed not through words and concepts but via an even more primal language of the body, made up of movement and physical gestures. Using a formal codified language of the body, movement was transmitted down through the ages via forms. The old masters revealed the secrets to their most trusted and worthy disciples.

Today the Tri-Harmony way of wellness emphasizes form practice as a vehicle for self development both for fitness as well as cultivating self-awareness. Adhering to the Principle of Three-in-One, Tri-Harmony unifies three elements:

1. A series of postures or body motions
2. Mental concentration
3. Breath control

In this book, the basic principles of Tri-Harmony are briefly introduced, and the essential form, the Universal Form, will introduced in detail, so that readers can begin to practice it immediately.

What is the Universal Form?

The Universal Form is a multi-dimensional health exercise that embraces physical fitness, meditation, and stress control. Based on traditional Buddhist and Taoist practices, this form strengthens and stretches the muscles, calms and clears the mind, and cultivates inner peace. In addition, it improves posture, while its movements promote deep breathing, enhance blood circulation and the functioning of internal organs. It is easy to learn and can be practiced at any time, anywhere, without special equipment. With the Universal Form all you need is yourself to develop yourself. With the Universal Form you can transform your stress into power or peace; you can energize or relax in just three minutes.

In terms of stress management, although it appears simple, the Universal Form is a versatile exercise that can be directed in a variety of ways; this is what makes it truly an original and useful routine. It can be done softly like Tai Chi, but it is more than Tai Chi; it can be done vigorously like a calisthenic but it is not limited to fitness. It can be done like a Qi Gong exercise for longevity. You can perform these easy rhythmic movements most simply as a powerful body-conditioning exercise for overall physical fitness, as a method of warming up or cooling down when you participate in other sports, as a tranquil moving meditation out in nature, or as a joyful flowing dance to express personal moods. Most practically, you can relax yourself or energize yourself immediately whenever you feel the need to.

As change propels us into an uncertain future, the Universal Form gives us a practical means of transforming stress to power or tranquillity, achieving personal harmony in the chaos of daily living.

What is Tri-Harmony?

Tri-Harmony is a holistic way of health for the next millennium. Neither the East, steeped in a profound spiritual tradition, nor the West, with its astonishing technological advances, has a monopoly on truth. Tri-Harmony developed out of the necessity of creating a new paradigm, a model for health based on integrating Eastern spiritual and healing traditions with Western science and medicine.

Today the holistic movement and integrative medicine endeavors to find an intelligent synthesis—and to avoid simplistic reductionism and the pseudo-scientific reasoning rampant in much New Age thinking—without bias for one over the other. Since each tradition has seemingly contradictory mindsets, rooted in extremely complex systems of knowledge that are truly difficult to reconcile, this is a formidable task indeed. It is certainly much easier to advocate such a synthesis than to actually implement it. Nevertheless, at the expense of ridicule and resistance, open-minded and patient pioneers from both the East and West have been experimenting with new, holistic paradigms of health and wellness, which are now beginning to receive more attention and respect.

Since the early days of the recent fitness boom, it has become ever more apparent that physical fitness and health, though related, are not necessarily synonymous. Many physically fit people, possessed of beautiful bodies and finely toned muscles, are unbalanced emotionally. On the other hand there are other individuals who are emotionally and mentally fit, but are underweight, overweight, or sickly. This disparity between mental and physical fitness reflects the traditional Western view of a distinct separation between mind and body. Spirit is rarely addressed.

What distinguishes Western sports and exercise from the Eastern forms of yoga and martial arts are different world views. The East applies a holistic approach to exercise whereas in the West there is the tendency to departmentalize and segment. Despite the purported character-building aspect of sports, we in the West rarely think of taking up basketball, golf, tennis, or jogging to become better human beings, or for cultivating higher moral values, or as a path of spiritual evolution. Mind and body and spirit are considered separate; academia and athletics are different departments in universities, while spiritual cultivation is almost ignored.

TRI-HARMONY in Chinese is *san he dao*. *San he* means "three-in-one," while *dao* literally means a "path" or "way," often referring to a way of thinking or a way of life. The words together denote a philosophy based on the perception of existence as composed of the tripartite realms of heaven, earth, and humanity.

In contrast are the Eastern disciplines like yoga, martial arts and Tai Chi, which all possess intrinsic philosophical and spiritual foundations underlying the physical arts, so that mere exercise or what we in the West conceive as sport is elevated to a way of life, not just rewarding pastimes or competitive passions that we engage in on weekends to keep in shape or to vent our aggressions.

Fragmented Being

The old notion of physical fitness has of late evolved into "fitness and health." For the physique there are jogging, aerobics, and weight training, while for the mind there are psychotherapy, yoga, and meditation. The popularity of all of these indicates that people are striving to keep both mind, body, and spirit in good health, but a separation between the three is still perpetuated.

Rushing off to a physical trainer or gym on Mondays, Wednesdays, and Fridays to keep in physical shape, going to see a therapist on Tuesday evenings for emotional health, and attending religious services on the weekend for our spiritual side is the standard ideal for maintaining personal well-being. However this demonstrates the fragmented approach to living.

Unified Being

In the Far East, this fragmentary approach to exercising the mind, body, and spirit does not exist, because by its very nature the mind is of, and inseparable from, the body. Chinese traditional Taoist and Buddhist thought teaches that what appear to be mutually exclusive, even contradictory opposites are, in fact, complementary; mind and body are thus different expressions of a single self. Likewise art, science, philosophy, and spirituality are parts of a whole and are embraced in each and every discipline, be it flower arrangement, architecture, healing, or painting. From this holistic view of life and its activities, it seems evident now that mind, body, and spirit must all be mutually maintained to achieve health and well-being. It is only through a disciplined method of discovering and developing our unconscious potential that wholeness of our being can be attained.

Consequently, the ideal aim of Tri-Harmony is to cultivate unified awareness, a centered state that is vital for the universal goals of achieving health, happiness, and success. What is called unified awareness is much more than normal awareness, which is typically fragmented consciousness. This unified awareness of our being includes the normally unconscious mental, physical, and emotional elements of ourselves, unfolding through the Tri-Harmony discipline that embraces:

1. Self-care: physical fitness and healing
2. Self-empowerment: psychological growth
3. Self-transformation: spiritual awakening

Balancing of Opposites

Unified awareness is not a permanent state of being, but rather an ideal that a conscious individual ceaselessly aspires to attain in order to grow toward greater self-awareness and to transcend his or her normal state of fragmented consciousness. It is important to remember that unified awareness is not an absolute; one doesn't, unfortunately, simply realize unified awareness and then suddenly find that stress and existential problems cease. There is a continuous, dynamic process of consciously balancing between the polarities of fragmented awareness and unified awareness.

Although one should not impose Eastern philosophies on Western lifestyles—the twain never have and never will meet—there is a lot to be learned from the holistic attitudes of the East that gave birth to Zen, a science of the mind, and Kung Fu, a martial practice for the body.

日　月

THE SHAOLIN HAND SALUTATION symbolizes in the clenched fist the sun, yang, and the martial way of the warrior. The open hand symbolizes the moon, yin, and the peaceful way of the monk. Harmony is attained when these opposites are balanced.

Shaolin Temple Roots

According to legend, the first patriarch of Zen, Bodhidharma, was also the originator of the Chinese martial arts as we know them today. This famous monk journeyed from India to China around the year 527 to pay a short visit to the devout Buddhist emperor, Liang Wudi, who had failed to grasp the deeper meaning of Buddha's teachings. The emperor was convinced that by good deeds alone one could earn karmic merit and attain Nirvana. Bodhidharma cryptically explained that the combined wisdom and purity of enlightenment could only be attained by penetrating into the "true nature of being."

Upon leaving the court of the emperor, Bodhidharma journeyed to the Shaolin Monastery in Henan, a revered place where monks were assiduously studying Buddhism. The patriarch noticed, however, that devout though the monks were, many of them were falling asleep while trying to attain enlightenment through long periods of meditation. Bodhidharma therefore introduced some passive and active psycho-physical

BODHIDHARMA is not only revered as the first patriarch of Zen Buddhism, but is traditionally considered the founder of Chinese martial arts.

exercises that complemented the severe mental and physical strain of intense seated meditation. These moving meditation exercises not only woke up the monks, but helped them achieve superior physical prowess and high levels of physical fitness.

These exercises, the forerunners of the modern martial arts, greatly improved the general health of the monks, which had deteriorated under the sedentary demands of meditation. Soon the shouts and cries of monks engaged in combat filled the silence of the serene temple courtyards. At the Shaolin monastery, both Zen Buddhism and Shaolin Kung Fu were developed as the monks strove to become enlightened through unified mastery of their mental, physical, and spiritual selves.

ZEN, called Chan in Chinese, is a sect of Buddhism that believes enlightenment may be attained by the individual through intuition and meditation.

Heaven, Earth, and Humanity

The warrior monks believed in a fundamental trinity at the core of all nature, the three interdependent forces or energies of heaven, earth, and humanity. A human being was a microcosmic representation of the universe, which was reflected in the components of the human self: the mental, the physical, and the spiritual.

Seekers of unified being thus took on tripartite identities, assuming the roles of the scholar (mental), the warrior (physical), and the monk (spiritual). Tri-Harmony uses this mythic model of the master to symbolize the ideal of a whole human being, the aware individual who has cultivated the capacity to self-regulate the three components to maintain complete mental and physical health. Time has proved that the monks were on the right track, and much of their teaching can be applied to our lives today.

Unifying Mind, Body, and Spirit

It is important to remember that Tri-Harmony is not an abstract philosophy but a holistic model of being, a way of developing a unified awareness of our total being—our mental,

THE MASTER symbol-
izes wholeness of
being through pos-
session of intelligence
of the scholar , the
power of the war-
rior, and the wisdom
of the monk. In turn,
the scholar, warrior,
and monk are
metaphors for the
three functions of
the self: thoughts,
actions, and feelings.

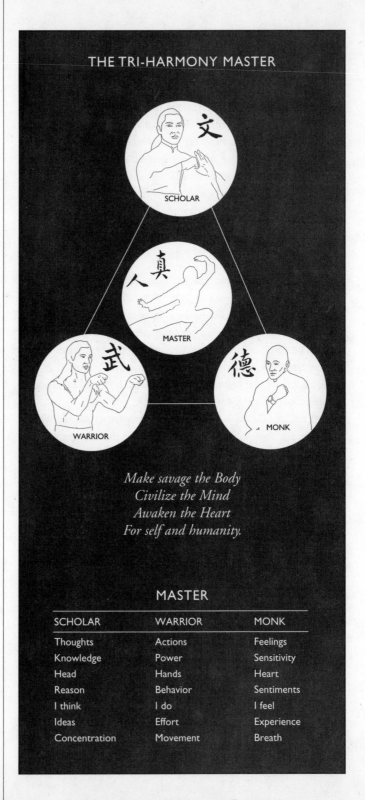

THE TRI-HARMONY MASTER

Make savage the Body
Civilize the Mind
Awaken the Heart
For self and humanity.

MASTER

SCHOLAR	WARRIOR	MONK
Thoughts	Actions	Feelings
Knowledge	Power	Sensitivity
Head	Hands	Heart
Reason	Behavior	Sentiments
I think	I do	I feel
Ideas	Effort	Experience
Concentration	Movement	Breath

physical, and spiritual selves. Tri-Harmony is based on the notion that our health and sense of wellness can be self-regulated to a much greater degree than we are normally accustomed to. The process begins by studying the normally unconscious interrelationship between the mental, physical, and spiritual aspects of our being. The practitioner then learns and develops conscious control over these three components through rhythmic tension and relaxation movements, and mental concentration coordinated with breathing. Finally, he or she internalizes the techniques and employs them when stressful moments arise. Studying Tri-Harmony principles and practicing the Universal Form are methods to help us consciously participate in the normally unconscious process of human growth.

As one becomes adept and sensitive to the mind-body-spirit relationship, one can easily apply the Tri-Harmony teachings to everyday life. Under stressful situations, whether trying to hail a taxi cab during rush hour or preparing for a big business showdown, one can either relax or energize through the muscle and breath control developed by the Universal Form.

For today's harried professional and urban dweller, trying to combat stress as well as maintain both mental and physical health, the ancient movement and meditation exercises of the Shaolin warrior monks may be just the solution for surviving, striving, and thriving.

*An enemy is as good
as a Buddha.*

—Buddhist saying

THE MASTER'S SWORD

Cleaving the air
my body develops power
to conquer my fears.

Focusing in space
my mind attains knowledge
to destroy my ignorance.

Penetrating the void,
my heart cultivates wisdom
to slay my ego.

Chapter 1

Ultimate Stress

I magine that an enemy is standing in front of you with a sword raised overhead, eyes glaring, fiercely determined to achieve one goal—to kill you. This is stress. At this critical moment, ozone depletion, nuclear war, illness, inflation, loneliness, and all other sources of anxiety become totally irrelevant. You are facing death. Here. Now. With a real existential problem: What are *you* going to do?

Sheer survival is your immediate goal. An error in judgment now may be the last error you will ever make. Such an error might mean confronting the ultimate unknown—death.

This hypothetical life-and-death crisis is a powerful metaphor for ultimate stress. Two opponents clashing in a death duel is clearly a dramatic comparison for the ceaseless conflicts and the relentless stress each of us encounters every day in our personal and professional lives. And yet, this is not an overly exaggerated analogy. Scientific research documenting the intimate relationship between stress and health reveals this most important fact: stress can kill.

What Is Stress?

Stress is a state of severe physical, emotional, and physiological tension induced by a threatening situation or an excessively frustrating experience. Under extreme duress the body automatically prepares for an emergency response. The muscles expand and contract, and the mind is alert for immediate action. Our whole being is ready to instinctively react, to fight or flee, without conscious thought.

This primal fight-or-flight reaction, when adrenaline pumps through our body, is nature's way of providing a quick burst of energy in order to escape danger. The response of early humans encountering a wild beast, or a warrior meeting a sword-wielding adversary, is similar to that of a contemporary person accidentally stepping in front of a speeding car in rush-hour traffic. When we are about to perform or speak before a large group we often feel queasy. The sensation of "butterflies in our stomach" is the body reacting to stress by producing adrenaline. If this state of nervous anticipation is not relieved, our ability to function normally becomes impaired.

Although the fight-or-flight response generates incredible strength, concentration, and power, it lasts only briefly, just enough time to flee from the animal, fend off the sword attack, or jump back from the oncoming car. However, if sustained for too long, the reaction strains and exhausts the body. Excessive physical preparation without release becomes chronic muscular tension and excessive alertness becomes emotional anxiety. Therefore stress in and of itself is not negative, it is natural. However, prolonged, unmitigated stress has an insidious (since it is often undetected) and debilitating effect on our bodies.

Problems of Stress

Whenever health and fitness are discussed today, stress is invariably mentioned. The relationship between stress, the immune system, and disease has been documented by researchers such as Dr. Hans Selye, who pioneered stress studies. When the mind and body are under continuous stress, the physiological effects of anxiety (muscle tension and adrenaline stimulation), intended for emergency responses, are actually debilitating to our health. Studies prove that stress impedes hormone secretions, which influence emotions. Stress suppresses normal body functions, making us more prone to ill health and accidents. Stress also reduces antibody production, which affects our ability to combat foreign bacteria and germs.

What Causes Stress?

Simply stated, life itself. Especially in this chaotic period when the pace of change seems to be accelerating so fast that we cannot keep up. Our modern urban lifestyle creates unrelieved stress. What we call "normal" is a state in which we are perpetually put in stressful conditions, induced by both personal and global problems. Even the time we devote to "getting away from it all" is stressful, as we deal with packing, unreliable transportation, waiting in line, and so on. Sometimes we even say, "I need a vacation to recover from my vacation," but instead of winding down after traveling, we rush off to work the next day, where we feel the stress of being "behind."

Our psychosomatic responses to life's challenges influence our health. The corrosive effects of prolonged stress on our minds and bodies are understood by modern medicine to be a major contributing cause to a multitude of physical and emotional maladies. These range from minor colds and depression to serious diseases such as heart ailments and mental illness.

As technology plunges us into an uncertain future, our lifestyle is now synonymous with accelerating change and relentless stress. It is no wonder, then, that life sometimes seems like a battle. Luckily, this battle can be won, if we arm ourselves with the understanding of how conscious balancing of the mind and body can effectively alleviate stress. We *can* take action to ensure our own health and well being. The first step is by studying both traditional Eastern and modern Western methods for coping with stress.

少林拳

The Tri-Harmony Solution

Tri-Harmony is a method for unifying the mind, the body, and the spirit by transforming the ubiquitous stress of our daily lives into power or inner peace. By integrating Zen and the martial arts from the East with psychology and science from the West, this modern approach is rooted in the twin disciplines that emerged from China's Shaolin Monastery, Kung Fu and Zen. But what does Kung Fu, an ancient esoteric fighting art, and Zen, an Oriental religion, have to do with effective stress management technology for people in contemporary life?

The challenge of human survival in a life-threatening confrontation against a skilled opponent was thoroughly explored by Shaolin monks. They began with the essential problem: How can I develop myself so that I can most efficiently survive? Ultimately, they came to believe, survival depended not on skill with the tools of combat, nor on military tactics or strategy, but rather on the individual monk himself. For even the deadliest weapon and the most ingenious fighting method were useless

unless the monk could overcome his own primal fear and urge to flee in the face of danger. Thus the solution to devising a superior response to a life-and-death confrontation had to be achieved by developing the total self.

SHAOLIN MARTIAL ARTS are indicated by the characters on the facing page.

The Triad Principle

According to traditional Chinese philosophy, all existence is comprised of a triad of forces or energies, those of heaven, earth, and humanity. Related to the individual, the heavenly force symbolizes spiritual energy, the earthly force symbolizes physical energy, and the human force represents mental energy. Harmony is achieved when the three forces are unified and aligned. Conversely, disorder and chaos, stress and illness, prevail when these forces are in conflict or not in balance.

The ancient Chinese martial arts masters sought to cultivate personal harmony by devising methods to unify and balance these energies inherent in every individual. Through unique

THE AUTHOR practicing Kung Fu with the warrior monks of Shaolin Temple.

psycho-physical exercises, they learned to develop the three incomplete components, then integrate them in order to unify the self. Further, these enlightened warrior monk found that the capacity to master a dangerous foe was nothing other than a way of mastering life itself. They naturally concluded, as should we: If I can develop and unify my physical, mental, and spiritual skills to protect myself in life-and-death confrontations, imagine how effective these same abilities will be in dealing with the stressful assaults in daily life, which for the most part are not immediately dangerous or life-threatening.

Tri-Harmony Synergy: the Principle of Three-in-One

Synergy is defined as an interaction that creates a whole greater than the sum of the parts. In other words, 1 + 1 + 1 is greater than three; it is four or more. Power is not just totaled, it is enhanced. Tri-Harmony Synergy, the principle of Three-in-One, is defined as the capacity to maximize power by unifying three separate forces into a single directed flow. How can a one-hundred-pound woman toss a two-hundred-pound man in combat? The application of the Three-in-One principle in martial arts makes this possible. The three forces at work in this case are the opponent's attacking force, the defender's force, and the force of gravity. Through skillful use of body leverage, the smaller women can unbalance and throw the heavier attacker, while thanks to gravity, the opponent's own weight will be used against him as he crashes to the ground.

Attributes of the Three Forces

In the Tri-Harmony model, synergy is created through the joining of a physical, a mental, and an emotional component. Each component has three functions:

1. A source of power
2. A mode of perception
3. A mode of communication

THE TRIAD PRINCIPLE

天
HEAVEN

地
EARTH

人
HUMANITY

Heaven and Earth and I are of the same root,
The ten thousand things and I are of one substance.
—Seng Chao

TRIAD PRINCIPLE

HEAVEN	EARTH	HUMANITY
(Spiritual Realm)	(Physical Realm)	(Mental Realm)
Inspired ideal	Material reality	Intellectual concept
Intuition	Instinct	Reason
Creative imagination	Pragmatic action	Logical thought
Unmanifested potential	Manifested energy	Manifesting energy
Super conscious	Subconscious	Conscious
Unconscious archtypes	Unconscious instincts	Consciousness
Wouldn't it be nice if...	The way it is...	The way it seems...
Sacred	Primal	Mortal

THE DRAGON in Chinese mythology is an auspicious creature able to roam freely through air, land, and sea. It thus symbolizes the Tri-Harmony ideal of an aware individual striving to develop spiritually, physically, and mentally. These three components of the whole person correspond, in the Chinese world view, to the energies of heaven, earth, and humanity.

The Cycle of Creation-Sustenance-Realization

Through our creative vision, sense of higher ideals, and sublime inspiration a thought seed originates. Our mental powers nurture this unmanifested ideal by planning and organizing; our physical power further implements this order and through sustained effort promotes growth. If our vision, thoughts, and actions are aligned the circle is completed, and a miracle manifests. What at one time did not exist flowers into a physical reality.

Whether the result is a poem, a relationship, a career, a family, or our lives, isn't this the universal process of creation? So, too, it can be with our health and our power to cope with stress. In order to create a unified power, the three forces—mind, body, and spirit—must be consciously aligned, integrated, and focused. Only through a process of intense practice, trial and error, and training can we cultivate alignment skills needed for maximize synergy.

Our Challenge

Although the principle of Three-in-One is easy to grasp conceptually, it is not easily achieved. Merely combining three distinct forces will not create synergy, just as merely mixing flour, water, and eggs will not make a cake. Besides the actual ingredients, knowledge of the right proportions, the mixing sequence, baking temperature, and timing are crucial for successfully baking a cake.

Like any other refined skill, developing Tri-Harmony Synergy requires study and practice. This is the result of a disciplined learning process in which we:

1. Identify and develop in isolation the individual components—mental, spiritual, and physical.
2. Integrate the three components through precise alignment.
3. Consciously direct and target this unified power to achieve specific results.

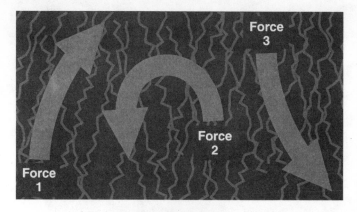

DISORDER AND WEAKNESS result from independent forces acting alone; their power is fragmented, and their energy is dissipated.

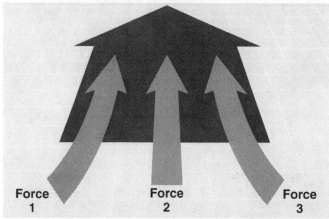

TRI-HARMONY SYNERGY results from the three forces acting in concert to create an even greater power than the sum of all three, the principle of Three-in-One.

Creating Tri-Harmony Synergy Power requires practice and patience before it can be cultivated. It is a challenge, and those who persevere will achieve great rewards for their efforts and time commitments. In the next chapter we will see how this principle of Three-in-One, or Tri-Harmony Synergy, will find practical expression in Tri-Harmony Centering, the basis of the Universal Form.

*We sit around a
ring and suppose
But the Secret
sits in the middle
and knows.*
—Robert Frost

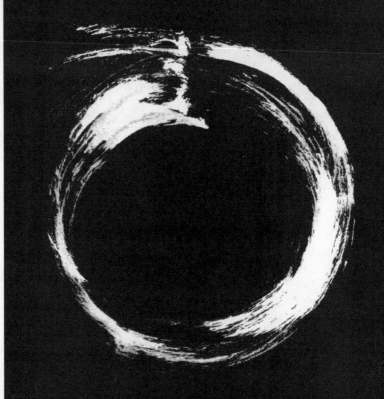

If my mind is too calm I become inattentive.
If my mind is too alert I become anxious.
When centering, my mind is calm and alert.

If my body is too relaxed I become lethargic.
If my body is too energized I become tense.
When centering, my body is relaxed and energized.

If my breath is too deep I become intoxicated.
If my breath is too soothing I become languid.
When centering, my breath is deep and soothing.

Chapter 2

Tri-Harmony Centering

High-level health and stress management are achieved through the art of centering, an expression of the principle of Three-in-One, also referred to as Tri-Harmony Synergy. The concept of centering echoes the traditional wisdom of both East and West: "Nothing in excess," reads the Greek aphorism inscribed at the Temple at Delphi. This concept corresponds with Buddha's Middle Path, the balanced course of action found between the opposite extremes of physical hedonism and spiritual asceticism. Both Confucius and Aristotle also emphasize the Golden Mean, the way of balance, in their writings. Clearly, both ancient wisdom and common sense indicate that our lives would be much improved if we could attain moderation and balance in our everyday activities.

Let us return for a moment to our imagined scenario of ultimate stress, an attack by a sword-wielding adversary. In this crisis situation, how does the reaction of the untrained individual differ from that of the Shaolin master? Most of us would be in a state of terror. Gripped by fear, physiological changes rapidly occur. The hair at the nape of the neck rises up, we

FRAGMENTED AWARENESS
manifests itself in the
problems of chaos,
conflict, and confusion.

A mind captivated by intelligent thought
—knowledge, words, ideas—
but ignoring feeling or action.
    A body seduced by powerful action
    —strength, skill, beauty—
    yet neglecting thinking or feeling.
        A heart intoxicated by emotional feeling
        —joy, sorrow, anger—
        while suppressing thinking or action.

begin shaking, our mouths become parched and adrenaline pumps through us; we are on the verge of losing control of ourselves. Like our bodies, the master's body may initially undergo the same physiological reactions. Unlike the untrained person, however, the master, demonstrating Hemingway's "grace under pressure" par excellence, is able to transform internal pandemonium into effective action. He is in control.

How does he manage this? By centering. That is, by consciously balancing both mind and body so they function in harmony, even under intense stress. And though he may initially react with panic—the master is human as well—he has the capacity to regain his emotional equanimity and respond naturally and spontaneously. With the ability to center, and thus to create Tri-Harmony Synergy, he can most efficiently coordinate and draw on his three components of being.

Awakening to the
stress, crisis, and discord of fragmented awareness,
I aspire to enlightened wholeness.
When the three separate forces
of hand, head, and heart
converge into a single directed motion.
With mute eloquence
my being flows through
time and space.

Normal is a Fragmented State of Being

We are rarely centered. Although the three components of being are interdependent, most of us do not utilize our full human potential. We habitually operate from a state of fragmentation of the mental, physical, and spiritual aspects of our selves. There is unconscious conflict within and without: conflict between our emotions and thoughts, between our spiritual aspirations and pragmatic actions, or between our internal selves and our external environments. The stereotype of the absent-minded professor, who is so immersed in profound thought and so oblivious to the immediate environment that he trips over the curb, is an example of someone who is fragmented. This fragmentation is also apparent when our feelings are in conflict with our actions and thoughts. It is possible to perform an activity very efficiently when we are mentally and physically coordinated, but if our emotions are not in accord, we are still not centered. Consider those who are highly competent and successful in their professions, but who are also unhappy and wish they were somewhere else doing something else. This is also an example of fragmentation. For centering, each fragmented part must be individually balanced within, and then integrated with the other balanced components.

Centering Is Unified Awareness

Centering is a dynamic state of being that exists when a person with a balanced mind aligned with a balanced body is totally immersed in the present moment. This state of unified awareness is synonymous with centering. Only rarely do we realize such a state, in ourselves or others, when we express ourselves or perform some act with excellence—unselfconsciously, effortlessly, gracefully, and efficiently. Such moments may occur in one's professional life, in sports or dance, while painting or playing music, or during the practice of any skill when the performer has become one with the activity and there is no separation between the performer and the action.

Achieving this total presence of being is rare, since it requires integrating mental concentration, spiritual attitude, and physical behavior on a higher level. In this ideal state, there is no fragmentation of being. The centered individual, therefore, has a threefold unity of being, of mind, body, and spirit.

Centering is Total Presence of Being

We are said to be centered when our unified being is immersed in the present while also in unity with the environment. Although a person may perform a skill well, to be truly centered he or she must be doing the appropriate action with regard to the environment. Painting a beautiful picture but being unaware that the house is on fire is not being centered. Just as centering is the harmonious relationship of the internal self

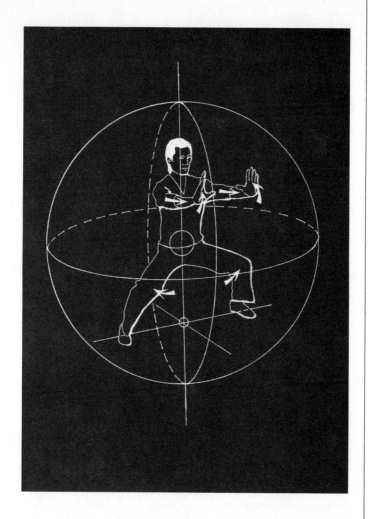

(emotions and thoughts) and the external self (actions and behavior), it is also the relationship between the self and the external environment. Think of an Olympic skier gliding down a mountain slope or a singer in an electrifying concert; both are totally in the present and in sync with what is going on around them. It is as if the skier and mountain are one, or the singer is one with the band and audience. Centering is not just the balanced individual in isolation; it is the balanced individual in action, action in accordance with the surrounding world. Centering is total presence of being unified by awareness.

CENTERING is refined balance. It requires the dual alignment of a balanced mind with a balanced body.

Centering and Balance

Although certainly related, the concepts of balancing and centering are not quite identical. We can be physically balanced yet not centered if our thoughts are wandering or our emotions are unstable. If we are physically feeding the baby while mentally preoccupied with a business transaction, we are not centered.

On the other hand, we can be mentally balanced yet still not centered if our body is ill or our posture is not aligned. For instance, we may be mentally balanced and absorbed in typing at a computer with our bodies slumped over in the chair. Again, this is not a centered state. Centering, then, requires the dual alignment of a balanced mind with a balanced body.

The Purpose of Centering: Being Here Now

Have you ever eaten a sumptuous meal in a special restaurant but failed to savor the food because you were preoccupied ? Or have you ever been with someone while thinking about someone else? Or have you been so busy running here and there on a vacation trying to see and do everything in a new country that you really weren't enjoying the sights? In these situations you were not *in* the moment.

The purpose of centering is to create an elevated integration of mind, body, and spirit in the here-and-now, thereby consciously changing our normally fragmented state of being. Just as in Zen, our ideal is to create an aware state of serene intensity in the moment. Instead of fretting about the past, which we cannot change anyway, nor obsessing over the future, which may never happen as we fear or imagine it will, we re-educate ourselves to be in a heightened state of consciousness so we can enjoy the present moment. In other words, we stop and smell the roses.

Whether feeling physically tired or emotionally negative, we can effectively alter our frame of mind or bodily state through centering. By learning to center we avoid being victimized by the personal and global problems that assault us daily, because we cease to obsess about and overreact to them. We are also more able to gracefully and efficiently confront the unknown challenges with which life confronts us moment to moment.

We empower ourselves when centering. Since unity is power, the normally fragmented and conflicting energies of our mind, body, and emotions operate together synergistically. With the ability to center, therefore, we have the capacity to consciously determine our own health and well-being, attaining a state of maximum mental and physical fitness. When centered, we are living at our optimum level. Mentally we are calm and alert. Physically we are relaxed and prepared. We manifest a vibrant spiritual attitude.

Centering is not a panacea that automatically solves all of our problems, however. Rather, through centering, we learn to respond to the challenges of life from a peak performance state, devoid of helpless despondency, lethargic apathy, obsessive emotions, or distorted perceptions. In time, we develop new and creative responses to personal relationships and to life's overall stresses.

When centered, we seem to surge with an abundance of energy, exude confidence, and generally feel good about ourselves. In this state, we tend to move with positive ease among others and treat people differently than when we are low on energy or lacking in self esteem or confidence. People naturally gravitate towards those who are centered. Therefore, while we work on changing ourselves we are indirectly changing how others relate to us.

The Three Actions for Centering

Centering affects as well our ability to solve problems. The centered person usually finds more creative solutions to the same problems that would create pandemonium in another person's life. For the centered individual, life and its inevitable conflicts and problems become exciting challenges instead of day-to-day crises, as they do for a less centered person.

Ultimately, it is not what happens to us that matters, whether good fortune or bad, but how we respond. For example, ideally one possessing the highest level of martial arts abilities will never have to use those fighting skills; the true martial arts master has the inner confidence to walk away from situations of impending conflict whenever possible, while another may also choose not to fight out of fear or cowardice. We may do the same thing for opposite reasons.

Centering helps us to gracefully and efficiently engage in the battles of everyday living. But how do we center? Life is movement. Indeed our spectacular universe is really only energy in motion. In the heavens are the movements of the planets, celestial bodies, and patterns of weather. On the earth there are the movement of the ocean currents, living organisms, and the seasons. Within every human being there are movements of body, mind, and spirit.

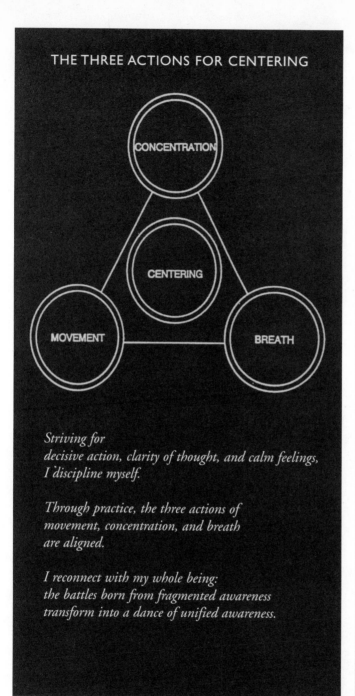

THE THREE ACTIONS FOR CENTERING

CONCENTRATION

CENTERING

MOVEMENT

BREATH

CENTERING is dependent upon three actions: movement, the form, must be practiced with the proper concentration and breathing techniques.

*Striving for
decisive action, clarity of thought, and calm feelings,
I discipline myself.*

*Through practice, the three actions of
movement, concentration, and breath
are aligned.*

*I reconnect with my whole being:
the battles born from fragmented awareness
transform into a dance of unified awareness.*

Centering is achieved through movement re-education. Specially designed moving meditation exercises, called forms, teach us how to become aware of and to refine fundamental movements that have become atrophied through disuse. Practicing these exercises while concentrating and breathing properly are the three fundamentals actions of centering. Together, these will strengthen and integrate the three components of our being—physical, mental, and spiritual—allowing them to act in unison.

1. Movement: Action of the Body

Mastering body movement is, of course, crucial for the warrior engaged in the business of life and death. Yet even for the peaceful monk aspiring to spiritual heights, the body has to be healthy and developed before it can be transcended. Similarly, strengthening and controlling the movements of our body and muscles is fundamental to centering. Action refers to movements of the body. These mechanical movements of muscles are the most obvious kind of motion of the human organism.

Since all muscles of the body have the impulse to action, it is through systematic relaxation and contraction movements that we learn to master our bodies. Daily practice of these structured movements is designed to develop a heightened sense of awareness of our musculature and skeletal structure. In short, we learn to control all the muscle groups of our body. This biomechanical sensitivity aids us in enhancing our physical being, a major step in centering.

2. Concentration: Action of the Mind

Observe a gourmet chef, a star athlete, a virtuoso violinist, or a martial arts master in action; all have mastered the art of concentration. For taming and channeling the turbulent movement of our minds is certainly a prerequisite for mastery of any discipline. Ancient wisdom, and again, common sense, suggest that our mind is both the origin of our problems and the source of liberation from them. Consequently, mental concentration is essential for centering. To achieve this rare ability to focus our minds despite the full spectrum of psychological fears, desires, anger, and suffering, we must learn to recognize conscious intentions and to target our energies toward specific purposes or goals. Just as the sun's rays focused through a magnifying glass can burn a hole through a piece of paper, or the concentrated energy of a laser beam can cut through steel, so too can learning to focus our mind's energy unleash tremendous power.

Therefore, mastery of the movements of the mind through concentration is a potent skill by which we can create the extraordinary from the ordinary. By focusing our normally scattered thinking and feeling, we have the ability to transform our stress, negative emotions, and problems into health, well-being, and a higher-quality life.

3. Breath: Action of the Spirit

Since ancient times, breath has been associated with the profound mystery of life itself. Both Eastern and Western traditions have linked breath with spirit. In the ancient teachings, breath, like spirit, is invisible but can be felt and can act upon things. Breath was observed by the ancients to the most vital element of human life. After all, a person can live weeks without eating and several days without drinking water, yet will die within a matter of minutes without breathing. Breath is so precious that, like spirit, it has been regarded as a sacred force.

The intimate relationship between breath and spirit is further evident in the esoteric concept of intrinsic energy, inner power or, most recently, as made popular in the *Star Wars* epic, the Force. This concept, known as *qi* in Chinese, *ki* in Japanese, or *prana* in Hindu, is also equivalent to the *pneuma* in Greek or *ruach* in Hebrew. As with yoga, Tai Chi, and martial arts, proper breathing and breath-control techniques are an integral part of centering.

BALANCE is the key to the art of living, and is represented in the ancient Chinese symbol for yin and yang, which together form Tai Chi, literally, the "Great Ultimate."

Centering: Balancing the Opposites

It is evident that many types of negative behavior, such as addictions to alcohol, smoking, drugs, gambling—all the so-

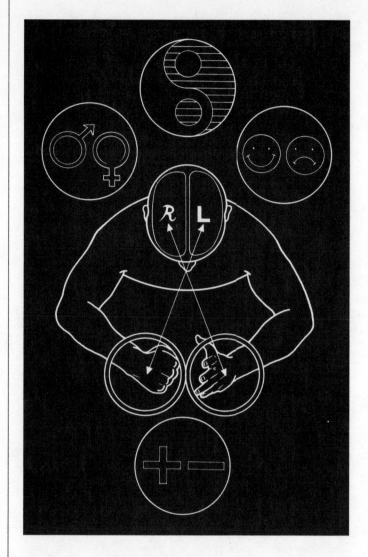

called vices—are destructive habits that undermine our physical and emotional well-being. Yet we often fail to realize that many seemingly positive actions can become excessive and create problems. There is the overly conscientious parent who becomes a workaholic to get ahead materially and fulfill the American dream, only to emotionally neglect his or her mate and children. Conversely, we find the parent who educates and emotionally nurtures his or her child but fails miserably to provide the material necessities. An excess of even what is considered "good" can lead to problems.

Cultivating balance is striving for moderation. We must try to avoid extreme indulgence, whether perceived as a vice or a virtue. However, true balance is never static. Everything in life changes, and from time to time we will again lose our balance.

Thus, pursuing permanent balance is an illusion that must give way to a ceaseless process of striving to regain equilibrium. This effort to maintain relative health is a lifetime process. Therefore, the subtle art of balance is the beginning: a secret key to living well. Balance is also the key to centering. In order to achieve centering, each of the three actions—movement, concentration, and breath—must be in balance between two opposite extremes.

1. Movement: Balancing Relaxing with Energizing

> *If my body is too relaxed, I become lethargic.*
> *If my body is too energized, I become tense.*
> *When centering, my body is relaxed and energized.*

One of the qualities that distinguishes a master from a novice in any art, sport, or field of endeavor, is the capacity to control relaxation. While the efforts of the beginner are often characterized by excessive exertion of force, evident in the inappropriate use of facial muscles, the truly adept use only the minimum amount of energy needed to get the job done. This economy of motion or conservation of energy is an attribute of the great performer, athlete, dancer, or martial arts master. The capacity to relax under pressure is crucial for superior performance. So, too, is relaxation fundamental to the art of living and the science of health.

The ability to control our muscles through relaxing and contracting provides a useful tool for controlling stress, anxiety, and tension. Yet excessive relaxation can make us too drowsy or lethargic. Although muscular tension is not negative in and of itself, when it becomes excessive it must be relieved. We must be able to control our muscles. So a key to balancing the body is maintaining a relaxed state while still being able to spontaneously contract the body muscles at the appropriate times and in the right situations.

In sports and physical activities that rely on power, this control is also crucial. The ability to effortlessly tense relaxed muscles at the point of contact generates explosive power effective for kicking and punching or swinging a tennis racket, baseball bat, or golf club. While the amateur tenses the muscles unnecessarily, believing that tensing the muscles increases power, the master employs economy of motion and relaxes the muscles until the critical point—then tenses. For daily stress management and centering, we should learn this important principle of economy of motion from the masters. We must train ourselves not to react spontaneously and emotionally to situations, but wait until our "emotional power" will be useful.

2. Concentration: Balancing Calmness with Alertness

If my mind is too calm, I becomes inattentive.
If my mind is too alert, I becomes anxious.
When centering, my mind is both calm and alert.

Both the way of contemplation and the way of action require the training of the mind. The monk quietly absorbed in meditation and the warrior in the heat of battle both seek a mental state that is calm and alert. Within a mind filled with scattered thoughts and emotions, we must seek that elusive critical balance point between calmness and alertness.

With a calm and tranquil mind, we are more capable of dealing with minor stresses; we can assess relationships and situations without the distortions created by emotional turmoil. When we are angry or upset we tend to view things negatively and are susceptible to reacting irrationally. For example, after being criticized by your employer earlier in the day, you may become enraged with your spouse, for no apparent reason, later that evening.

On the other hand, being too calm may result in our becoming too passive. We know of those people who are so

CENTERING is an ultra-refined balance, requiring the alignment of a balanced mind with a balanced body.

calm and "laid back" that they procrastinate and fail to act when the situation demands it. Too much calm can result in apathy and impede quick reactions in emergencies. Thus, in addition to being calm, we must strive to be totally alert. Yet, at the same time, being over alert to problems and situations can create a state of anxiety or, at a greater extreme, paranoia. Centering is attained only when there is an equilibrium between calmness and alertness.

3. Breathing: Balancing Inhalation with Exhalation

> *If my breathing is too energized, I becomes intoxicated.*
> *If my breathing is too soothing, I becomes languid.*
> *When centering, my breathing is both energizing and*
> *soothing.*

As the yoga, Zen, and martial arts masters discovered long ago, conscious control of inhalation and exhalation is a powerful tool for creating a centered sense of being. There are numerous breathing techniques, some well known and others the jealously guarded secrets of various schools and sects. In some, inhalation and exhalation is balanced; some emphasize inhaling, while others emphasize exhaling or even holding the breath. Some use the mouth, others only the nose while breathing. No matter which variation, breath control is vital for centering.

Learning the technique of balancing inhalation and exhalation is the key to controlling our physiology. Inhalation brings oxygen into the bloodstream which enriches and energizes all the cells of our body. By inhaling deeply we fuel ourselves. Exhalation, on the other hand, removes the carbon dioxide waste from our body. Naturally there should be a balanced cycle of fueling our bodies with oxygen and eliminating toxins.

The natural breathing cycle can change many times during a day depending on our internal state. When we are angry, frightened, or upset our breathing pattern is usually shallow, agitated, and quick. Perhaps you've found yourself gasping for breath when you've received shocking news or if you've ever had to speak in public or perform before an audience. Here, the stress and fear has affected your normal breathing patterns.

When we are happy or peaceful, however, our breathing is smooth deep, and rhythmic. Perhaps you remember times when you've found yourself inhaling pure fresh air while walking along the ocean or standing on a mountaintop gazing at the sunset. Or you may have listened to the deep and rhythmic sounds of a child or a lover in a blissful sleep. Breathing reflects our inner state. Therefore when centering we consciously employ the relaxing, rhythmic breathing patterns we associate with a state of tranquillity and happiness. Centering is balancing opposite states:

> *When concentrating the mind is calm and alert.*
> *When moving the body is relaxed and prepared.*
> *When breathing the breath is soft and deep.*

Centering is Unified Awareness

Centering brings a heightened consciousness of the vast spectrum of experience that in our normally fragmented state we are not conscious of. It is through this heightened consciousness that we become aware of when we have become unbalanced. By identifying which area is in a state of imbalance, we can then compensate for it, much like deciding to do more sit-ups in the gym or be more conscientious about our diet on Monday after a weekend eating splurge.

Centering is subtle. Imagine a tightrope walker constantly making minute adjustments of his balance as he crosses the wire. Centering also requires awareness of the many polar extremes as well as sensitivity to their relationships, which are always changing. Mood swings, happy to sad, angry to depressed, will affect our stress levels positively or negatively, as will our physical state, whether we are hungry, fatigued, or ill.

Besides the relationship of physical and psychological factors in maintaining healthy equilibrium, it is necessary to realize the equally important intimate relationship we have with the external world, especially the myriad external factors that we cannot control: the weather, problems in professional, personal, or family relationships, business and political ups and downs, and ecological problems—all are intricately connected with our sense of well-being. Part of centering is to know when it is advantageous to control the situation and when to let go and allow the external situation to dictate to us what to do. We must train ourselves to stop being needlessly anxious; when there is nothing we can do to solve a problem, we must learn to go with the flow.

With the ability to regulate the influence of each polarity, we can center at will by concentrating on synchronized rhythmic muscular movements coordinated with rhythmic inhalation and exhalation. When practicing the Universal Form, we will continuously strive to balance opposite qualities: our minds should be calm and alert, our bodies should be relaxed and prepared and our breathing should be smooth and deep. The benefits of the daily practice of the Tri-Harmony centering and the Universal Form will be personal serenity, harmony, and health.

Returning to
Nature's way—
Transforming Stress
to Tranquillity

*The new humanity will be universal, and it will have the
artist's attitude; that is, it will recognize that the immense
value and beauty of the human being lies precisely in the fact
that he belongs to the two kingdoms of nature and spirit.*

Chapter 3

The Universal Form

The Tri-Harmony approach to health and fitness teaches centering through three stages:

1. Practicing the Universal Form
2. Understanding the principle of centering
3. Applying centering techniques in daily activities

The Universal Form is a centering exercise that engages our entire being, allowing none of the fragmentation of the body, mind, and spirit that is common to various conventional forms of exercise. Many activities we engage in, even those we undertake to make us healthier, express our customary state of fragmentation. If, for example, we are jogging through the park listening to music on a headset, our bodies are being exercised but our minds are tuned out. Or else we can be mentally engaged in watching a movie or reading a book, but not exercising our bodies, and even oblivious of their existence. Finally we can be emotionally absorbed in rapturous music while ignoring completely our bodies and our conscious thoughts.

These activities that isolate one or two components of our being may be beneficial in and of themselves. Yet the problem of not having enough time in our hectic schedules creates the need for a single form of exercise that embraces our physical, mental, and spiritual components. The Universal Form does this.

What is the Universal Form?

The Universal Form is body conditioning, meditation, and stress reduction integrated into a single exercise. As an expression of the key Tri-Harmony principle that unifies mind, body, and spirit in a manner that promotes health and centering, the form coordinates three actions:

1. Physical action
2. Mental concentration
3. Rhythmic breathing

This natural health method embraces physical and psychological fitness and promotes a general sense of well-being. Simply put: the goal of the Universal Form is high-level health. Unlike most other exercise methods or sports there is no need to rely on equipment, weights, uniforms, a special practice court or any external paraphernalia we need only ourselves. With the Universal Form, we use the self to develop the self.

The Roots of the Universal Form

As related in the Introduction, an enigmatic figure named Bodhidharma is revered, somewhat paradoxically, as the legendary founder of both Zen Buddhism, a way of self-liberation, and Shaolin martial arts, a way of self-defense. After observing monks falling asleep during the long rigorous periods of seated Zen meditation, he devised a series of active and passive psycho-physical exercises, the Muscle Changing Method, and a form called Eighteen Monks Boxing, in order to improve the frail health of the monks.

These moving meditation exercises are regarded as the embryo from which Shaolin martial arts evolved. Although training was initially for promoting health and spiritual cultivation, eventually these meditative postures were transformed into ingenious fighting techniques. Such a prearranged series of fighting techniques that can be practiced solo is called a form.

To be sure, most people study martial arts for self defense. As a result, violence and physical conflict, though not the original aim of health and self-development, are often associated with martial arts. This unfortunate, because many people who would otherwise be afforded a fascinating path of self-discovery and self-development do not undertake the study of these excellent mind-body exercises. They are unaware of the tremendous rewards of health, inner peace, and increased energy that martial arts practice can provide, as well as the simple, but exhilarating joy of movement.

The Universal Form is a method of centering, a concise mind-body exercise that has benefits of the Muscle Changing Method attributed to Bodhidharma. Unlike the original movements, a series of isolated exercises that can be rather tedious to perform, the movements of the Universal Form are integrated into a single exercise. The Universal Form is more readily adaptable to our contemporary lives chiefly because it requires far less time to practice. A form of three repetitions can easily be completed in five minutes or less.

The Universal Form is easy to learn and once learned can be modified in various ways to suit one's personal health and fitness needs. Further benefits of the form can be achieved by employing Tri-Harmony centering techniques that are derived from the form. These practical centering techniques can be practiced anywhere and at any time.

Benefits of the Universal Form

> *Give me health and a day,*
> *and I will make ridiculous the pomp of emperors.*
> —Ralph Waldo Emerson

The entity we call a human being is one of nature's most profound mysteries: an intricately organized biological organism that has evolved over billions of years, a microcosm of the universe and an enigmatic being comprised of a physical body, a reasoning mind, and a third, elusive component called spirit. Such is Shakespeare's "man, the thinking reed," this organic bridge between the material and spiritual realms, a spiritual animal born from marriage of the twin forces of heaven and earth. The Universal Form is an exercise method encompassing these various aspects of our biological and psychological being.

Mastery of the Universal Form directly enhances basic psycho-physical skills: strength, movement awareness, muscle and breath control, coordination, and concentration. Daily practice of the Universal Form will provide numerous benefits, the most important of which are examined in detail below.

1. Better Posture

> *As long as the soul stands erect it holds the body high*
> *and does not allow the years to touch it.*
> —Nikos Kazantzakis

Our posture, the habitual way we carry ourselves when standing, sitting, or walking, not only reveals a great deal about us, but also determines our physical, mental, and emotional state of being. An erect carriage and proper alignment of the body can have an extremely beneficial influence on our overall health. Since the head, which constitutes ten to fifteen percent of the body weight, is delicately perched on top of the slender rod called the spinal column, bad posture can adversely affect head, neck, shoulders, and back.

Proper alignment and flexibility of our spinal column is essential for good health since the efficient functioning of our central nervous system, which transmits electrical impulses throughout our bodies to our brain, is related to our posture. All the nerves of our spinal cord passes through vertebrae that make up the spinal column. Our habitual posture or unconscious movements can thus interfere with normal activities.

Chronic poor posture as a result of either standing or sitting unnaturally gradually creates faulty alignment and loss of function. This shifting of the vertebrae into unnatural positions and adding excessive pressure on the spinal disks causes inflammation of nerves passing through the spinal column. Furthermore, as the misalignment becomes chronic and habitual, our body learns to compensate for the imbalance.

When our bodies are out of balance, excessive wear and tear is placed on the joints, muscles, tendons, and body parts that are compensating for the imbalances. In addition, there is stress caused by gravity pulling down on our muscles, bones, and internal organs day in and day out. When this force is coupled with abnormal alignment, numerous injurious effects may result: the transmission of nerve impulses to the brain may be dulled, thus impairing five senses, agility and flexibility may be reduced, movement may be hampered, and functioning of our internal organs may be made less efficient.

A major benefit of the Universal Form is that it can be used to improve poor posture. Over time, daily practice of the Universal Form (under trained supervision, focusing on correct postural alignment), can naturally and gradually adjust chronic spinal misalignment. With consistent repetition, we will cultivate a heightened kino-esthetic awareness and re-educate our bodies to move habitually with an aligned posture while standing, sitting, walking, or running. This will increase our tolerance to stress.

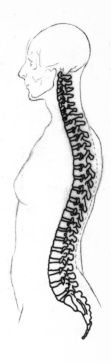

THE SPINAL COLUMN should be flexible and properly aligned for good health.

2. Greater Flexibility

Flexibility is enhanced through stretching. We stretch naturally; indeed, upon awakening from sleep we typically begin our day with a sensuous cat-like stretch. A systematic stretching program, the importance of which is recognized in today's sports training, has been the key to ancient health and hygienic practices from the East, such as yoga from India, and exercises imitating animals from China. If there is a single secret exercise for health, it is stretching; a supple body is not only a more graceful body, but is healthier because it resists injury.

MAINTAINING FLEXIBILITY both of the body and the mind is a secret to aging gracefully.

As we age, it is more important to maintain flexibility than develop greater strength, since flexibility promotes the energy flow within the body. Doing the Universal Form increases temperature and blood flow to the muscles being stretched; it elongates the muscles, increases their range of motion, and improves overall flexibility. The five arm-extension positions of the Universal Form utilize each muscle group in all planes, extending each muscle to the extreme in each direction.

Flexibility helps provide the speed for quick bursts and fast movements. Since a pre-stretched muscle resists stress better than a unstretched muscle, stretching reduces the risk of injury and enhances our athletic performance. As a pre-sport warm-up, the Universal Form is an excellent way to prepare the body for a strenuous activity like running, skiing, tennis, or swimming. It is also a wonderful way to cool down after a workout or sports activity.

Stretching awakens our kino-esthetic awareness as we focus on and feel the various areas of our bodies performing the movement. We get in touch with our bodies. Finally, the best reason for stretching is the simple pleasure of stretching itself—it feels good.

3. Increased Strength

To be strong is one of the primary and most typical goals of fitness training. In addition to the improved appearance provided by well-developed and well-defined muscles, being strong eases the burden of everyday tasks like carrying and moving things, or climbing flights of stairs. However, although the importance of strength in athletic endeavors is assumed and understood, its influence on overall health is often overlooked. Vigorous strength training can lower blood cholesterol levels, burn fat, aid cardiovascular health, and reduce blood pressure and average heart rate.

The Universal Form has been designed to exercise virtually every muscle group and one hundred percent of the muscle fiber through alternating tension and relaxation movements. Chief benefits of the form will be increased strength and improved muscle tone, and ultimately the development of long sinewy muscles and tendons similar to those associated with a swimmer's physique.

Unlike other sports exercises that use the muscles in a random manner, the Universal Form utilizes both the agonistic and antagonistic muscles in a balanced manner. The extension and contraction of each movement employs the full range of the muscles. And since individual muscle groups are isolated during different parts of the form, we develop muscle awareness and control. Over time, we can control individual muscle groups at will. This ability is helpful particularly if you wish to work on the development of a specific muscle to enhance your performance in a particular sport. For example the Universal Form can develop strong and sinewy forearms which are so vital for sports like tennis, baseball, martial arts, etc.

4. Improved Breathing

Since breathing is one of the three essential elements of the Universal Form, its breathing techniques are naturally designed to benefit the respiratory system, which is chiefly responsible for the cyclic oxygen-carbon dioxide exchange throughout the body. The deep rhythmic inhalation and exhalation from the diaphragm and lower abdomen pumps oxygen-enriched blood throughout the body, fueling and energizing all the cells. At the same time, the build-up of carbon dioxide waste is flushed out of our bodies as we forcefully exhale.

5. Cardiovascular Fitness

One of the major keys to good health is the maintenance of the proper circulation of blood throughout the body. The bloodstream is the central system for transporting oxygen, nutrients, and hormones to different parts of our body while at the same time removing carbon dioxide, lactic acid, toxins, and waste. If our circulation is poor or impeded, our bodies either lose much needed energy or suffer from an over-accumulation of waste.

Practicing the Universal Form enhances the circulatory flow of blood throughout the body through vigorous or gentle back-and-forth motions of the arms. Doing the form correctly increases the blood flow to extremities, which can help reduce the discomfort associated with rheumatism and arthritis.

6. More Limber Joints

Just as we oil the hinges of a door to make it open and close more smoothly, it is essential to keep the joints of our body in "well-oiled" condition. Blood, hormonal secretions, and electrical impulses of the nerves all must flow smoothly to and through the joints, where they may be divided and redirected to initiate, fuel, or control muscular motion.

The circular patterns of the Universal Form stimulate the release in our joints of synovial fluid, our body's natural lubricant and one which dries up as we age. As well, all the joints of the body—toes, ankles, hips, waist, shoulders, elbows, wrists, fingers, and neck—are exercised when performing the Universal Form. When practicing the Universal Form, bear in mind that in order for them to function efficiently, all the joints of the body should be extended naturally, never hyper-extended and never held rigidly.

7. Better Balance

Balance, surely a candidate for a "sixth sense," is fundamental for optimum biomechanical functioning. Balance is closely related to correct body alignment, and is important in helping us to maintain correct posture. Since a symmetrical skeletal and muscular structure functions more efficiently, good balance helps us conserve energy, and reduce wear and tear on the muscles, joint, and bones. Moving from stance to stance while performing the Universal Form is an excellent way to improve both dynamic balance and static balance.

8. Improved Coordination

Coordination is the skillful integration of a number of separate physical and psychological factors: neural, muscular, and motor skills, speed, flexibility, balance, agility, sensation, and awareness. Because of the need to develop the mental concentration required for coordinating breath and movement, the Universal Form teaches us the most bio-mechanically efficient ways of using our body and muscles. Over time we can continue to refine these specialized movements through awareness of and utilization of specific isolated muscle group, enhancing our ability to control them. With this enhanced ability we learn to expend less energy for maximum stability, a skill beneficial in all sports and daily activities.

9. Calmer Nerves

The nervous system is an intricate electrical network running through out our entire body. It functions as the primary transmission system for carrying the impulses and messages from our five senses to our body's center of control, the brain. Our nervous system receives information from inside and outside the body and directs the movements of the limbs and sensory organs. Practicing the slow, rhythmic, meditative Universal Form quells the chaotic sensory bombardment our nervous system is typically undergoing. Our nerves become soothed and we return to a tranquil state.

10. Reduced Anxiety and Depression

As stated earlier, attention to the three actions for centering— how we move, how we breathe, and how we concentrate our minds—can dramatically change our physiology. When practicing the Universal Form, the chemistry of the brain is actually altered. In particular, morphine-like neuropeptides called endorphins, the natural opiates of the body, are produced. It is well known that exercise, especially involving rhythmic repetition, such as jogging, can induce a state of mental and emotional euphoria as endorphins are released, which reduces pain and produces sense of pleasure; the Universal Form operates in a similar manner.

11. Stronger Immune System

Regular practice of the Universal Form can strengthen the body's natural immune system, helping to ward off colds and other common illnesses.

When standing, stand.
When sitting, sit.
Above all, don't wobble
　　　　—Zen saying

POSTURES are components of forms; they are structured ways of aligning and moving the body.

Postures

Shaolin martial art techniques are executed through various postures that employ specific stances and hand positions. Although they can be interpreted as offensive and defensive movements, the initial intent of these postures were not martial in nature. On the contrary, each posture was originally a posture of meditation. For fundamental to both the martial arts and the discipline of yoga are static and dynamic postures, the aim of which is centering.

Postures are balanced body positions that facilitate a calming of the mind through rhythmic breathing. The Universal Form is comprised of various postures that change from one into another in a pre-arranged sequence. Postures teach us centering through proper muscular and skeletal alignment and the most biomechanically efficient way of moving. As a structured way of aligning and moving our limbs, postures are designed to re-educate our bodies to move more naturally.

Why do we need some artificial technique or exercise to teach us how to move? Don't we move naturally already? Ideally, of course, we share with animals the natural ability to move, breathe, and feel. For humans there are four natural postures: standing, lying, sitting, and walking. Due to our modern lifestyles, however—slouching in easy chairs, sitting up at our desks, wearing shoes on our feet while walking on pavement rather than grass, etc.—our natural postures have been altered. Basically, to accommodate our modern lifestyles, we have had to adapt to ways of walking, sitting, and standing that wreak havoc on our posture and spinal alignment. Learning scientifically structured postures, arm positions, and stances is a method of retraining ourselves mentally and physically so that we begin to move naturally once again. Before beginning the Universal Form itself, let us review the hand positions incorporated into its various postures.

The Five Basic Hand Positions

The Universal Form utilizes five basic hand positions, corresponding to the five directions or planes through which our muscles move. By extending the hands in each of these five directions, we employ the full range of motion of the muscles; thus we are able to exercise all the muscles groups and one hundred percent of the muscle fiber.

THE BASIC HAND POSITION is formed by bending all but the two index fingers, which remain straight.

Although the physical fitness benefits of the Universal Form are most obvious, the exercise is also a meditation for the mind. Here the benefits are more profound, but at the same time, more subtle. As originally conceived by the Shaolin warrior monks, forms are books of knowledge that used body movement and gesture as non-verbal language. Esoteric spiritual knowledge was communicated and transmitted through the forms. Unfortunately, although many practitioners today are aware of the physical interpretation of martial forms, they are "illiterate" with regard to much of the other information the forms can convey.

1. Moving Ahead (Forward Push)

CONSCIOUS ACTIONS are symbolized by this hand position. These are actions that we make and direct with conscious intention.

2. Moving Peripherally (Side Outward Push)

UNCONSCIOUS ACTIONS are symbolized by the the side outward push. These are actions that we do not perceive directly yet nevertheless profoundly affect us.

3. Grounding to Earth (Downward Push)

PRACTICAL ACTIONS are symbolized by the third hand position. Its downward-pushing action directs our energy and strength to the earth so that we ground ourselves, not only for physical stability but for stability in daily life.

4. Reaching to Heaven (Upward Push)

SPIRITUAL ASPIRATIONS are symbolized by the fourth hand position, an upward push toward heaven.

5. Balancing Rhythm (Side Downward Push)

RHYTHMIC BALANCE, which can be found in each and every moment of life if we train ourselves to be aware of it, is symbolized by the fifth hand position.

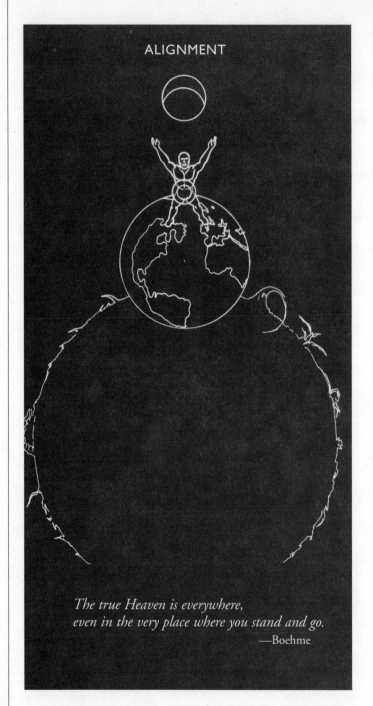

ALIGNMENT of the body and proper posture are crucial for good health, since gravity exerts a powerful pull on our muscles, bones, and joints.

The true Heaven is everywhere,
even in the very place where you stand and go.
—Boehme

The Universal Form

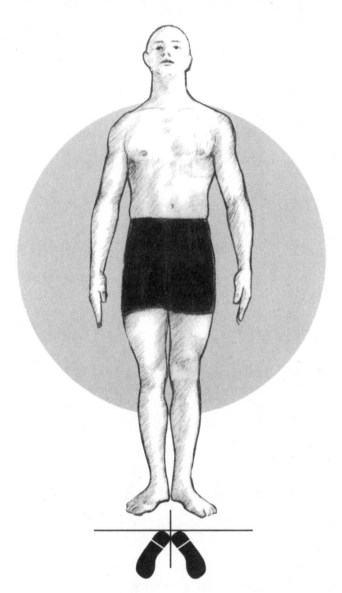

1. Begin centering as you assume the ready posture, shown at left. Stand at attention, heels touching and toes pointing outward. Your shoulders should be relaxed, chest out, spine straight, and chin tucked in slightly. Imagine a golden cord attached to the top of your head pulling you heavenward. Except for the upward tension that maintains your spine erect, you should relax completely, as if you were a puppet dangling from a string. Your arms and hands should feel heavy, and your eyes gaze straight ahead. Your breathing should be smooth, deep, and rhythmic.

An animated version of the Universal Form may be viewed via the internet at www.triharmony.com

2. Inhale as you circle your arms upward from your sides. Continue until your palms touch each other over your head. Clasp your thumbs together with your fingers pointing up. Stretch upward and feel the stretch.

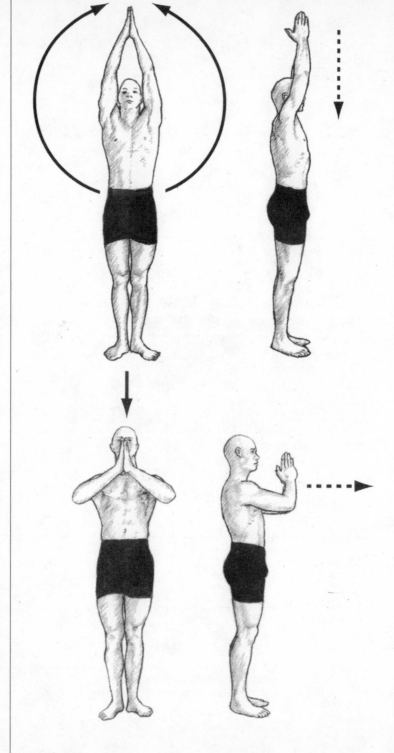

3. Exhale as you lower your hands together in from of you, as if in prayer. Feel the heat generated between your palms. Hold this position as you inhale. There is no hand movement accompanying this inhalation.

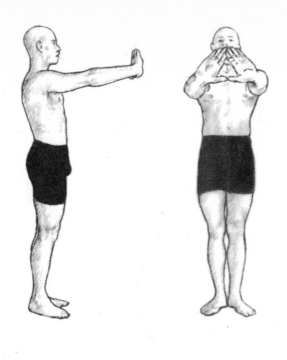

4. Exhale as you extend your arms straight in front of you. The tips of your right and left forefingers and thumbs should touch each other and form an equilateral triangle. This salutation symbolizes Tri-Harmony.

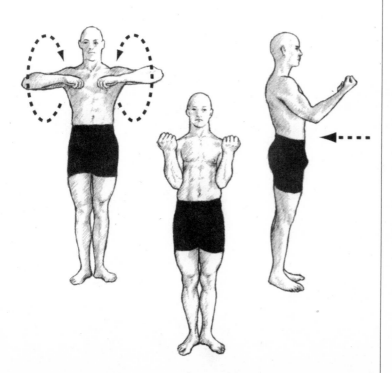

5 and 6. Inhale as you clench you hands into fists and draw them in to the front of your chest (5). Continue to inhale as you turn over your fists (shoulder height) and lower your elbows, as if you were holding a barbell in the curl position in front of your chest (6).

7. Exhale as you draw your fists back to your hips, brushing your forearms against your sides. Draw your elbows together as if trying to make them meet behind your back. Feel the tension in your upper back muscles.

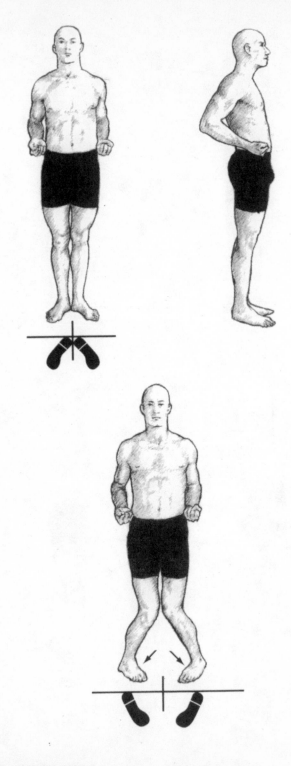

8. Inhale as you raise up your heels, and pivot on the balls of your feet as the heels move outward. Exhale as you bend your knees and stand in a pigeon-toed position. Feel the stretch in your hips and thighs.

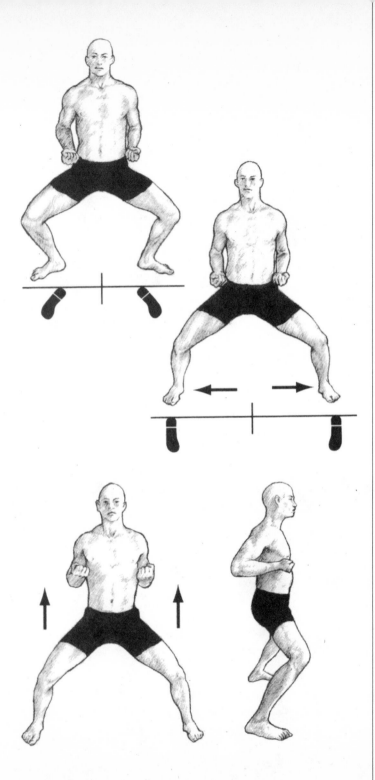

9. Inhale as you lift up your toes and pivot on your heels, turning the toes outward. Exhale as you bend your knees and sink your weight onto your feet.

10. Inhale as you lift up your heels and pivot on the balls of your feet, with the feet parallel, toes pointing straight ahead. Exhale as you bend your knees and sink down as if you are straddling a horse. This is called the horse stance.

11. Inhale while drawing your fists up your sides until your forearms are parallel to the floor.

12 and 13. Hold your breath as you open your hands, turn and point your fingertips down to the floor (12). Pivot them around until the fingertips point upward (13).

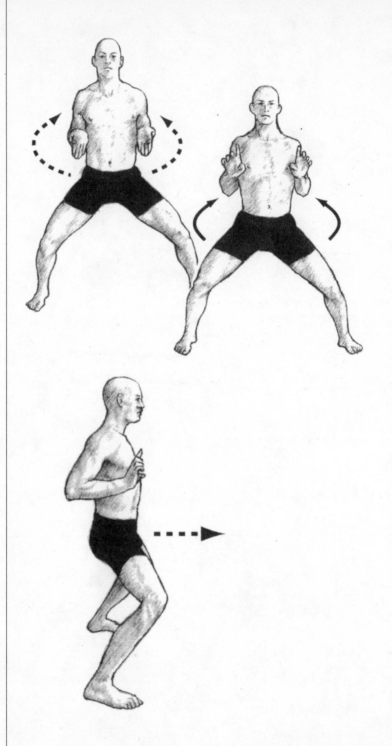

Hand Position 1

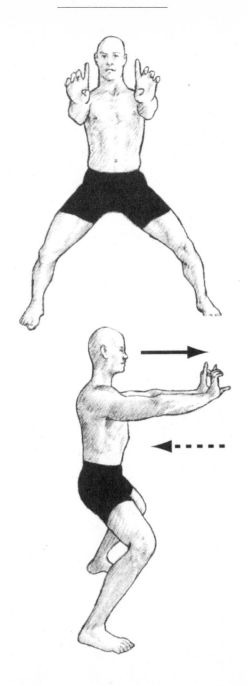

14. Exhale as you extend your hands out straight in front of you. From this position do three to ten repetitions: inhaling as your draw your arms back to your sides (13) and exhaling as you push them forward (14). Be sure your forearms brush against your side as you execute these movements.

15 and 16. Hold your breath as you turn your hands inward, palms facing out, and fingertips pointing toward each other (15). Inhale as you raise your arms from straight out in front of you until they are over your head, palms skyward (16).

Hand Position 2

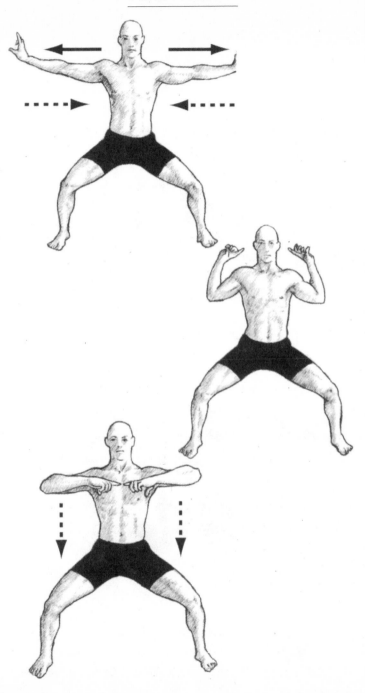

17 and 18. Exhale as you lower your arms to your sides. From this position perform three to ten repetitions, inhaling as you draw your palms inward (17) and exhaling as you extend them out to the side (18) as if pushing against two walls.

19. Hold your breath as you bring you arms in front of your chest.

20 and 21. Exhale as you push your palms downward in front of you. From this position perform three to ten repetitions, exhaling as you push down (20) and inhaling as you bring up your arms palm upward (21).

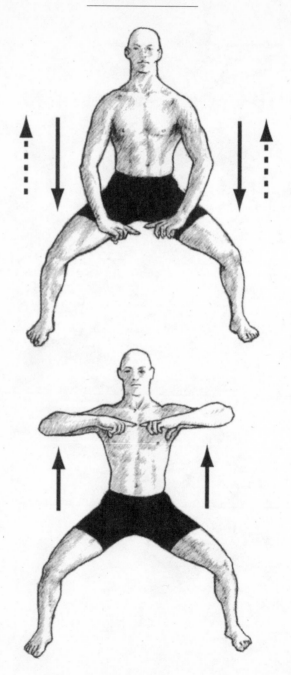

Hand Position 4

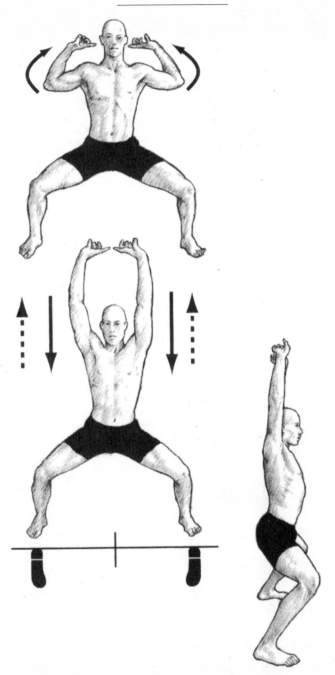

22 and 23. Inhale as you continue to draw your hands up from (21), and turn palms upward, fingertips pointing toward your ears. Exhale as you perform three to ten repetitions, exhaling as you push up (23) and inhaling as you lower your hands to your shoulders (22).

24 and 25. Inhale as you circle your arms inward and downward (24) and then extend the arms to the sides (25).

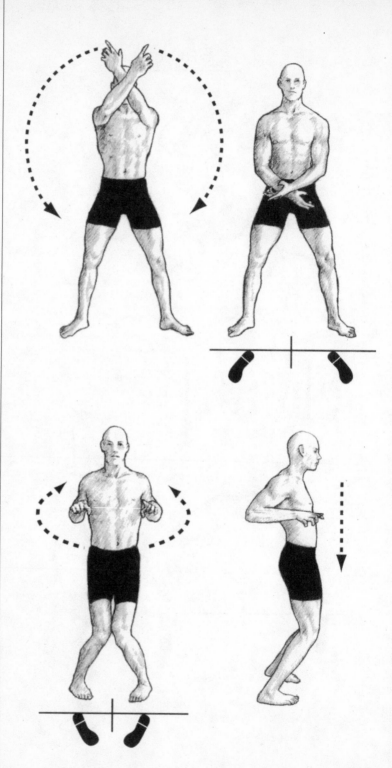

26. Tuck your hands to your sides in an hour-glass position with both feet pointing inward.

Hand Position 5

27. Exhale as you lower your arms at your sides, keeping your hands parallel to the ground. Do three to ten repetitions: inhaling as you draw your arms up along your sides and exhaling as you push downward.

28. Inhale as you circle your arms up from the sides until your palms touch your head in a closing salutation.

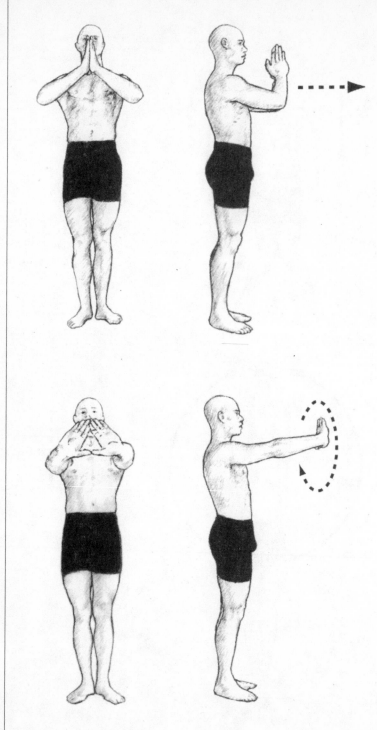

29. Exhale as you lower your arms to a prayer position in front of you. Then, holding the hand position, inhale without any arm motion.

30. Exhale as you extend your hands out in front of you, forming an equilateral triangle.

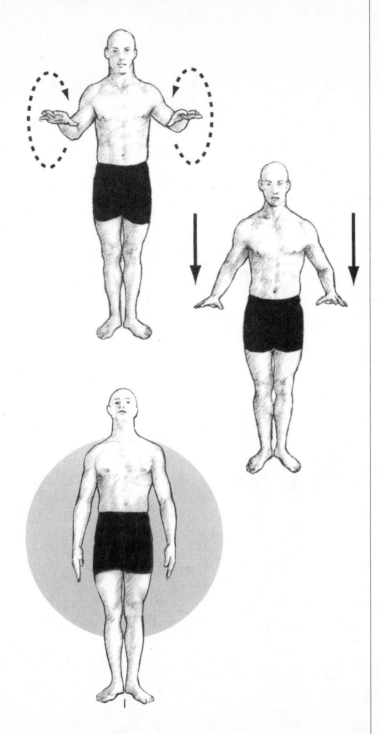

31 and 32. Inhale as you circle your arms downward and then out to the side (31). Draw them in toward your sides (32).

33. Exhale as you lower your hands to your sides. You are centered. Close your eyes and meditate for a few moments. Feel relaxed and energized.

Chapter 4

Variations of the Universal Form

After learning the Universal Form's sequence of movements, we can begin to explore several variations in its execution. Over time, we discover that varying these movements and postures can achieve different results. How we actually do the form will depend on whether we want to focus on body conditioning and muscle toning for physical fitness, or meditation and relaxation for stress reduction.

Intention Determines Execution

If we observe two people practicing the Universal Form, we might assume they are getting the same result, or at least have the same goal. However, depending upon the depth of their understanding and their reasons for practicing, different goals and results are possible. For one person the form may be just a type of calisthenics with the benefits essentially physical and aerobic; for another person the form may be a meditative exercise in which one is moving in harmony with the environment.

As it regulates all three actions for centering discussed earlier, movement, concentration, and breathing, the Universal Form can be utilized for either physical fitness, or meditation for stress reduction. However, targeting a specific goal will give the best results.

Physical Fitness

Unless you have thoroughly drenched yourself in perspiration, You can not expect to see a palace of pearls on a blade of grass.
—The Blue Cliff Record

The ideal of being strong and having a powerful physique undoubtedly goes back to the dawn of history when human survival often depended on the sheer brawn required to hunt wild animals and war against other tribes. Our fascination with both the aesthetics of the human form and its function is evident by our interest athletics, dance, and even film stunts; all demonstrates our respect for the superbly muscled and powerful, well-toned body.

Although a scientifically designed program of weight training is the most effective way to develop muscle bulk and great strength, this method requires time, equipment, and complete dedication. However, for those who are interested in a simple overall body conditioning exercise that strengthens and stretches all the muscle groups, the Universal Form is the solution.

Progressive Resistance Training

In order to focus on physical fitness, muscle toning, and body conditioning, the Universal Form must be performed emphasizing progressive resistance. Progressive resistance is an exercise method that gradually increases the difficulty of each movement by increasing the muscular exertion necessary to execute the motion. This conditioning taxes the muscle groups in order to build strength and create muscular definition. Weight training is, in fact, an example of progressive resistance exercise.

IRON WIRE is the Chinese metaphor for strength combined with flexibility, the goal of the strengthening method of the Universal Form.

Dynamic Tension

Those who are familiar with weight training will notice that some arm movements in the Universal Form are similar to those used with a barbell or dumbbells. Naturally, this means that the same muscle groups are being exercised. It is true that the Universal Form does not look strenuous, but appearances can be deceiving. When properly executed, with the body properly aligned and using dynamic tension, this exercise is very fatiguing to the muscles. In fact, bodybuilders are often astonished by how taxing this exercise can be when correctly practiced.

Unlike weight training, the Universal Form uses the body itself to create its own resistance by having the muscles oppose each other. This is called dynamic tension. Dynamic tension is created when complementary muscle groups, both agonistic and antagonistic, work against each other. For example, when we draw our fist toward the body or do a flexing motion, the bicep muscle is employed while the tricep is passive. On the other hand, when we extend our fists outward from the body, the tricep muscle is employed while the bicep is passive. With a dynamic tension movement, both the biceps and triceps are used to resist one another.

The secret to creating great muscular force is the proper alignment of the hands and arms. Unless the precise arm and hand placement is used throughout the extension and contraction of the movement, it is difficult to feel the alignment and, therefore, the proper tension. If it is easier to create resistance with weights, why should one practice the Universal Form? It must be remembered that the Tri-Harmony approach to self-care uses the self to develop the self. Understanding how to use our own body to develop strength provides us with deeper insights into how our muscles operate. Simultaneously, the Universal Form also helps us develop mental concentration since we must focus our minds to create the resistance of dynamic tension. By isolating individual muscle groups we learn to better control our bodies and cultivate a sensitive kino-esthetic sense that is not possible through weight training alone.

Iron Wire

Because the Universal Form both stretches and strengthens the muscle, the body develops a flexible, tensile, and wiry strength, more like the physique of a swimmer than that of a body-builder. The more supple muscles of the swimmer or martial artist are more efficient for ordinary sports and daily activities than the bulked up muscles of the weightlifter. A traditional Chinese martial art form called the Iron Wire is an appropriate description of the ideal of power, strength, and flexibility wedded together. Another description in martial arts is "iron wrapped in cotton." Here hardness (strength) is concealed in softness (sensitivity). This is the strength that the Universal Form can develop if practiced diligently and consistently.

Practicing for Strength

Practicing for strength requires intense mental concentration on the muscle being exercised. Movements should be done slowly and intensely, exerting maximum muscular contraction. It should feel as if the muscles are fighting one another, with one set of muscles (agonistic) trying to extend the arms and the opposing set (antagonistic) trying to prevent this. The muscles of the arms are the most obvious place to begin concentrating, since they are always in motion. Mentally focus on your triceps when you extend your arms; focus on the biceps when you retract your arms. Later on, pay attention to the muscles in your forearms.

Coordinating your breathing with each motion is also important. When doing these dynamic tension movements, your breathing should be strong and deep, coming from the lower abdomen. It is important to strongly tense your stomach when exhaling. Also it is important to squeeze your buttocks when exhaling. Breathing is slow and deep, smooth and forceful. When inhaling, we use the nose to breathe; when exhaling we use our mouths to expel the air.

Whenever we exhale, we must concentrate on tensing the muscles of our abdomen, chest (pectorals), and upper back (lats). Initially, it may be difficult to control these muscle groups. Start by focusing on tensing the abdominal muscles when exhaling. After this can be accomplished without conscious effort, try to focus on tensing the chest muscles along with the abdomen. After this becomes easy begin focusing also on the upper back muscles. Finally, concentrate on tensing the neck muscles. Mentally visualizing the muscle group being exercised helps build these muscles. In time, and with practice, all the muscles of the torso, arms, and legs can be controlled at will.

The Universal Form must be practiced strenuously to develop powerful muscles. Since this is a natural exercise, tremendous muscular resistance can be created by the body itself, without weights or equipment. Various muscle groups of the body work in opposition to one another through the relaxation and contraction of the agonistic and antagonistic muscles. In addition, precise hand placement is used throughout the extension and retraction of an entire arm movement. Hence, specific muscular and skeletal alignment and correct body mechanics facilitate dynamic tension. Dynamic tension can be created in several ways depending upon how strenuously you want to exercise. Following are three body conditioning methods.

1. The Aerobic Method

The aerobic method executes all arm movements with open, relaxed hands, using little or no dynamic tension. This variation of the Universal Form is done at a quick, brisk pace as if you are jogging or doing jumping jacks. It is thus an excellent aerobic exercise that promotes circulation, warms the muscles, and gets the heart pumping.

To further facilitate an increased heart rate, you should drop into the horse stance when extending your arms and raising up your torso by standing up. Do not lock your knees. When you inhale, withdraw your arms to your body. This squatting action builds up the thighs. Be careful not to drop too low if you have knee problems. Employ more repetitions (10–20 reps for each posture per set) and more sets (4–6 sets). When first learning the Universal Form and when first beginning body conditioning it is best to use the open-handed method. This is an excellent warm-up exercise for any other sport or activity.

2. The Stretching Method

The stretching method for physical fitness is performed at medium speed and is more strenuous on the muscles than the aerobic method. The muscle fiber is alternately relaxed and contracted. Open your hand while exhaling and extend your arms; clench your fists while inhaling and drawing your arms towards your body. There is a softer tension with the open hand and a harder tension with the clenched fist. Pause at the end of each movement. Holding each breath so as to consciously emphasize stretching in the direction the muscles are moving. This mild dynamic tension makes the Universal Form a wonderful and soothing stretching exercise that also is good for strengthening the muscles and tendons. Remember: s-t-r-e-t-c-h s-l-o-w-l-y and feel the movement.

3. The Strengthening Method

The strengthening method of body conditioning uses only the clenched fist for both pushing-out hand extensions and pulling-in hand retractions. This is the most strenuous of the three physical conditioning methods. It utilizes maximum dynamic tension and requires coordination and intense mental and physical concentration. In order to achieve maximum results, a smaller number of repetitions are used.

As you get stronger, it is possible to increase the difficulty of the exercise by isolating each of the five postures and exercising each arm position separately. For example, you can begin with three sets of the first position followed by the rest. Then go on to the second posture and do another three sets. Rest. Proceed to the next position until you go through all five postures. Then you can do another round. This separation of the arm positions allows you greater concentration on the muscle group being exercised. Finally, for even more tension, practice the movement with only one arm at a time.

Repetitions and Sets

When practicing the Universal Form for strength and conditioning, schedule a specific number of repetitions and a specific number of sets just as you would do in weight training. Gradually vary the number of repetitions and increase the number of sets for progressive resistance training.

To begin each practice, it is best to do a set of high repetitions (10–12) with quick motions to warm up the muscles, getting your heart pumping and blood flowing through the body. The second set of medium repetitions (6–8) can be done using the stretching method to slowly build up tension. The final set will utilize the strengthening method (5–6 repetitions each position). Again, for maximum resistance do three repetitions, noting that smaller numbers of repetitions require more concentration and exertion than higher reps, when the mind tends to wander. To end each practice, you can perform a relaxed open-handed Universal Form to cool your body down.

As you increase in strength, add more repetitions and more sets. Experimenting with the three variations of the Universal Form through practice will eventually help you find the most appropriate routine for yourself.

Meditation

The mind is a muscle.

—Yvonne Rainer

Legend tells us that Bodhidharma, secluding himself in deep meditation, could hear ants scream. Meditation is a way of accessing our unconscious by penetrating the veils of our everyday mind. A gateway to new experiences and of cultivating hidden powers of the unconscious mind is open to us through meditation.

Consider meditation as something like push-ups for the brain. Just as the consistent incremental repetition of push-ups develops muscle strength, disciplined practice of meditation enhances mental functions. While spectacular feats of physical prowess like smashing stones may demonstrate the warrior arts, the real power of the Shaolin monks was cultivated through the rigors of Zen meditation.

The Universal Form is not only an excellent conditioning method for physical fitness, it is also an effective moving meditation. By shifting attention to the subtle movement of breath rather than to the more obvious movement of the muscles during practice, the Universal Form as a conditioning exercise is readily transformed into a meditation technique.

Why Meditate?

Meditation has only recently begun to receive attention for its potential medical benefits, perhaps because it has been so long thought of as only an esoteric spiritual practice. Presently meditation in a secular guise, divorced from the original spiritual context, is being introduced as a medically sound relaxation technique, useful, for example, in treating high blood pressure.

Meditation is a natural relaxation method, requiring no drugs or medication. Without delving into its spiritual dimensions, we can all benefit from its basic aim of calming and clearing the mind.

Today, more and more emphasis is being placed on the psychosomatic nature of illness; some doctors even believe that all

illness is related to the mind, and that it is only when "psyche" (mind) and "soma" (body) are in equilibrium that we are truly well. In order to be healthy it is not enough to be physically fit; we must be mentally and emotionally fit as well. Indeed, the important mind-body relationship determines our health and cannot be ignored. Since the mind and the body are intimately interrelated, physical exercise alone cannot achieve mental harmony and health; we must exercise mentally.

The Mind is a Drunken Monkey

"The mind is a drunken monkey" is an Eastern aphorism that vividly describes the nature of our everyday mind: a conflicted mind, perpetually plagued by scattered thoughts, emotions, worries, desires, disappointments, and countless other distractions. One instant we feel one way; the next instant, we feel another way. Clearly we are not always in control of our minds. Indeed at times our turbulent psyche threatens to control us.

A simple experiment demonstrates this. Can you focus on a simple thought without being interrupted by another thought for a full minute? Sound easy? Try it. Try looking at the second hand of a watch, see how long you can repeat to yourself this single thought: I am here now . . . I am here now . . . and so on. You may be surprised to discover that you have difficulty focusing on that single sentence for even half a minute. For most of us, other thoughts and ideas rudely intrude: "What am I going to feed the kids for dinner? I forgot to send that fax! This is silly . . ." This is what is meant by the "drunken monkey," our ordinary mind. Reflecting on it, we see that our normal state of mind may be overburdened by excessive intellectualizing, self judgment, and ambivalent, uncontrollable emotions. All may rob us of our natural spontaneity and cause us to make poor decisions.

This being so, we habitually misperceive our relationships with others. Because our inner being is not in touch with our external environment, there is conflict between what we say and what we think. For example, you may disagree with your boss but still tell yourself it's best to agree. Or there is conflict between what we feel and what we think we should feel. (I may know, for instance, that I should be polite but I feel too angry).

Our conflicted mind is deceived by our fantasies and misinterprets reality. Our mind's drunken monkey reels between the plethora of polar emotions: desire and fear, joy and sorrow, love and hatred, pleasure and pain. Similarly, it continually fluctuates in its evaluation of practical thoughts, moral values, and creative ideas. And perhaps most dangerous is its propensity for destructive self-criticism, self-judgment, and fear of failure. Life is hard enough without berating ourselves needlessly for falling short of some perhaps impossibly high standard of per-

*When we quiet the mind,
the symphony begins.*
—Anonymous

fection. All this inner turmoil creates stress of which we are often dangerously unaware.

Cultivating a Mind like Water

In contrast to this habitual state of mental and emotional chaos, the drunken monkey mind, is the centered mind or meditative mind. A "mind like water" is the Zen analogy for a serene mind. The perfect reflection of the full moon on the still surface of the pond symbolizes a clear and calm mind in harmony with its surroundings, the highest level of mental cultivation. Moreover, as the slightest breeze rippling across the water will distort the moon's image, so do conflicting thoughts and emotions disturb our minds and distort our perception of reality.

When, for example, you might have found your toddler's behavior playful one day, the next day, after a run-in with your boss, you might suddenly find the identical behavior in the child obnoxious. Obviously our emotional states can influence our perceptions of reality. Only when our mind is utterly calm are we centered, and able to see with clarity. So, how do we stop the incessant chattering of our rational, monkey minds in order to center? How do we still the mind and make it tranquil? The answer is meditation.

Meditation is Intuitive Awareness

The phrase, "words and books on Zen are like legs on a snake," is to remind practitioners that even the most erudite and learned discussion of meditation will always fail to convey what it actually is. Moreover, such intellectualizing is ultimately irrelevant. To be sure, the "concept of meditation" and "meditation" are two different things. One is an idea and the other is an experience. Even the best description of a meal on the menu cannot satisfy our appetite. Meditation is not to be understood but to be experienced.

Cultivating the meditative mind, then, is not achieved through reading books or studying. It is not accomplished through the rational mind, by thinking, or by any effort of our conscious intelligence. On the contrary, it is achieved by turning off the over-developed intellect in favor of another type of awareness: it is done by tuning into intuitive awareness, the deeper, more primal mind.

What is intuitive awareness? A common psychological model of the human psyche or mind has divided it into two parts: the conscious and unconscious. The conscious mind is our thinking mind that analyzes, reasons, calculates, registers emotions, and remembers. It is usually what we call the rational mind or intellectual awareness. Usually, this rational self identifies itself as the center of our being, what we refer to as the "I" or the ego-self.

Through the ages, however, thinkers and seekers have realized that there is another dimension to our being, a deeper self hidden within. It is the unconscious aspect of our psyche, sometimes referred to as the inner self, that is capable of intuitive awareness. It is also called the unconscious, subconscious, or subliminal mind. Although not necessarily identical but somewhat similar, in spiritual language this non-conscious awareness has been called Christ-consciousness, Buddha-mind, the higher self, the God within, etc.

Rational awareness and intuitive awareness are in fact two different modes of perception. The former is perception associated with our conscious faculties: intellect, logic, and reason, expressed through language. The latter is perception via the unconscious, including instinctive processes of the body and mental functions that do not rely on intellect and which are communicated non-verbally to our conscious mind through images and intuition. Dreams, hunches, visions, and fantasies are examples of intuitive awareness.

A serious problem of modern men and women is that we are often one-sided or overdeveloped in favor of the rational mind. Nevertheless, the rational consciousness is but one facet of our psyche. As our rational awareness spends time analyzing, calculating and deciding, another kind of awareness is perceiving, our intuition. But it is non-conscious, non-rational. It feels rather than thinks. Yet it is still awareness through the unconscious. Meditation is a method of tapping into the latent powers of the unconscious.

CENTERING, for those who are intuitively aware, is seen a process of continual realignment that helps us maintain a beneficial correspondence with the physical and spiritual forces of the universe.

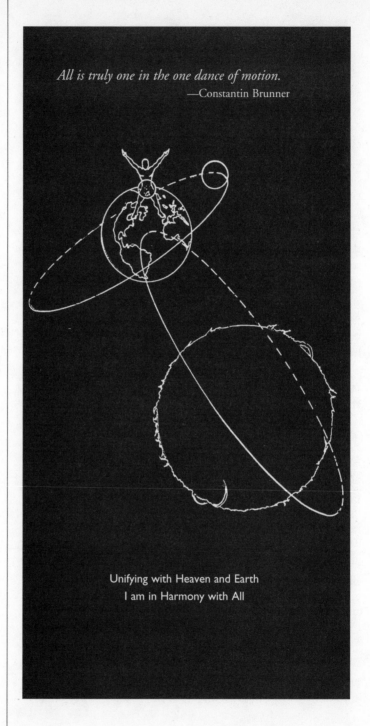

All is truly one in the one dance of motion.
—Constantin Brunner

Unifying with Heaven and Earth
I am in Harmony with All

THE UNIVERSAL FORM

The power of intuitive awareness is evident as we drive along the highway immersed in conversation or in deep thought without conscious awareness of steering, of the traffic, or even of the road. Although our conscious rational mind is occupied, we are still able to drive. Another example of intuitive awareness is expressed when we engage in an activity in which we are proficient; excellence in performance is often achieved only when the rational mind relinquishes control. Similarly, in artistic endeavors such as painting, singing or dancing, or even cooking, we are best when we "let go" or "go with the flow."

This quality activity occurs without deliberate or conscious effort; it is a result of the trained unconscious, the centering that results from a highly developed intuitive awareness. In such moments time seems to stretch. Sitting by the seashore mesmerized by the waves, or being immersed in an engaging conversation, or those peak experiences (being in "the zone") while playing golf or basketball are all examples. When mind, body and spirit are aligned and totally immersed in the task at hand you are in a meditative state of centering.

Unfortunately, most contemporary lifestyles emphasize rational consciousness, and we allow our intuitive awareness to atrophy. We have become unbalanced in favor of rational awareness at the expense of intuitive awareness. Meditation is a method to rectify this imbalance.

Intuitive awareness is achieved through unity of mind, body, and spirit. Time spent meditating yields precious moments of awareness devoid of conscious awareness or the overbearing rational intellect, the ceaseless self-critical internal dialogue, and the endless choices and pressures of conflicting emotions and desires. Meditation is the liberation of the unconscious mind. It unshackles the fetters of civilization and allows us to feel and express our intuitive self.

Centered Presence

When practiced as a meditation, the Universal Form is a potent method of stilling the drunken monkey in our mind, calming ourselves emotionally and relaxing our hyper-tense bodies, in short, centering. By making our minds crystal clear and our hearts tranquil, we are brought closer to a meditative state of inner harmony.

The purpose of meditation is to make the mind completely in the present, the so-called here and now. In addition to tranquilizing the chattering monkey mind that distorts our perceptions of the present moment, a meditative mind totally immersed in the moment can help us become aware of certain limiting behavior patterns. Since we are creatures of habit, we think, feel and do things according to patterns developed and conditioned over the years. For most daily activities, acting habitually, automatically, is efficient since it requires little or no conscious thought. As well, such unconscious behavioral patterns create security and familiarity.

Habits become limiting, however, when they perpetuate automatic responses no longer appropriate to a given situation, preventing us from having new experiences and thus restricting our personal growth. This is especially so when the habit is based on an old fear. How often have we decided that we cannot do something because we have failed in the past? Perhaps we experienced pain, humiliation, or guilt because of that failure. Therefore, when we encounter a similar situation, we automatically avoid it.

A meditative or centered mind can free us from becoming victims of limiting habits. When practicing the Universal Form, we engage our entire being by focusing on the three actions for centering: movement, concentration, and breath. Emancipated from past fears, desires, and prejudices that we normally project onto the present moment or project onto an imagined future, we can experience the present moment fully, as it is.

How to Meditate

While sitting meditation is often regarded as the supreme meditation technique, many beginners may find it too difficult and boring to simply sit cross-legged and "do nothing." Moving meditations are thus a practical means for those who find sitting too disciplined.

Meditation in motion utilizes physical movement as an aid to achieving a tranquil mind. When one is extremely tense, it is extremely difficult, perhaps impossible, to sit in a lotus position and try to cease all conscious mental activity. Moving meditations like Tai Chi and the Universal Form are both wonderful ways to rechannel nervous or excess energy. It is physical movement, the rhythmic contraction and relaxation of the muscles, that distinguishes sitting meditation from moving meditation. At the same time, the Universal Form is excellent for loosening and preparing you for sitting meditation or to rejuvenate your circulation between sittings. The following points should be noted when applying the three actions for centering, previously discussed, to meditation using the Universal Form.

1. Movement

Perform all the movements slowly, the slower the better. If it takes you an hour to do a single form, that is fine. When meditating it is impossible to move too slowly. Execute the form smoothly and fluidly, without any jerky motions. Everything should flow continuously. Finally, relax, relax, relax. When doing the physical movements use the minimum amount of strength necessary.

2. Concentration

Focus your eyes on a fixed point in space. Do not allow your eyes to wander. Gaze into the distance. Although meditation endeavors to stop the rational mind from thinking, the mind must nevertheless stay concentrated. How does one do this in order to free the intuitive awareness? By focusing the mind on the synchronized breathing with each physical motion. This brings us to the key technique for stilling the turbulent mind—breath control.

3. Breath

The key to breath control is correct technique: rhythmic breathing that is smooth, deep and slow. Breath softly—feel as if you are gently sipping fresh air from a straw. Breath slowly, the slower and deeper the better. Consciously focus on the quality of your breath, smell the freshness as you take in deep drafts of air. Breathing can actually take on a sensuous feeling.

The unity of the three actions centers us. By mentally concentrating on synchronizing rhythmic physical movement with breathing, we engage our entire being, drowning out all distractions by reducing our mental focus on a single rhythmic motion. Our being returns to the primordial rhythm. There is a confluence of three forces into one movement. The movement becomes the moment.

Stress Control

Let us live happily, then, free
from all ailments among the ailing!
—Buddhist saying

Imagine, you now have in your possession a three-minute defensive routine to fight stress: the Universal Form. Because it is simple and can be practiced anytime and anywhere, it is especially good for those who do not have a regular exercise routine. For those who do exercise, it can be employed as a supplemental activity. When practiced properly and consistently, it is an effective preventative measure against the ravages of stress.

It is important to recognize how stress actually affects our energy levels. No matter what the cause of stress, our energy is affected in one of two basic ways: either we experience a lack of energy when we are tired or excessive energy when we are hyper-tense. Managing stress is simply finding an effective way to control this energy imbalance and re-establishing a harmonious state of being. We learn to energize when we are tired and relax when we are tense. The Universal Form is how we do this.

To Relax or to Energize?

Before you can use the Universal Form for stress control you must determine which state you want to achieve. Do you need to relax or to energize? Revitalize yourself or calm yourself down? After identifying which state you want to attain, you can then use the appropriate method to compensate for either energy imbalance. To energize, employ the body conditioning method; to relax, use the meditation method.

When correctly practicing the Universal Form, our total being is thoroughly engaged in a single activity. By shifting our mental attention to the fundamental motions of breath, muscle, and mind, our normally overactive conscious intellect is absorbed in the rhythmic movement of the moment. Therefore we cannot think of anything else and normal self-consciousness decreases.

This moving meditation provides respite from our mental and emotional burdens. By temporarily forgetting the stress-inducing problems, anxieties, and inner conflicts that assail us daily, we take refuge within ourselves to re-center our being; we energize and relax by honoring that part of ourselves that had been neglected. We disengage, regain our balance, and return to our natural state of equilibrium.

It is important to realize that doing the form itself will not magically solve any problems; they will still be there after you practice. But there will be a crucial difference: you will be centered. Your mind and body will be aligned. You will be physically refreshed and will feel better. Your mind will be clearer and your attitude will more positive.

Returning to your problems from a centered state of being, you will regain perspective and avoid making errors that more often occur when you operate under extreme stress. Centered, you can confront and resolve the same problems in a more energetic, resourceful, and creative state of mind.

1. To Energize

Movements are dynamic
Concentration is intense
Breathing is forceful

Physical or emotional fatigue can be relieved by employing either the aerobic or dynamic-tension methods of executing the Universal Form, or a combination of the two. Either will clear your mind and revitalize your body. If you are lethargic, enervated, or depressed, performing the physical-fitness method will generate energy and make you more alert. To energize, perform the Universal Form with deep, rapid breathing and quick, alternating contraction and relaxation of the muscles. The deep breathing pumps oxygen into your lungs and the quick movements get your heart beating and circulate the oxygen-enriched blood.

2. To Relax

Movements are relaxed
Concentration is calm
Breathing is soft

If you are hyperactive, anxious, nervous, or angry, the Universal Form should be practiced using the meditation method. This will quiet your mind and relax your body. When you are emotionally overwrought and stressed, your muscles feel tight and knotted. Muscular tension usually accumulates in the neck, shoulders, and back. Although you know you need to relax, very often you find it impossible to suddenly relax on cue; few people can. If this is the case, you should first perform a dynamic-tension Universal Form before doing the meditation method. By consciously exerting the maximum muscular contraction possible, your already overly tense muscles will tire out. Then when you perform the meditation method, your muscles will relax naturally, out of sheer exhaustion.

Relax completely when moving. Use only the minimum strength necessary to move and avoid any excess muscular tension. All of your joints—fingers, elbows, wrists—should be naturally curved and slightly bent, not stiff or over-extended. Your limbs and hands should hang naturally. Cultivate the sensation of floating. Feel as if you are moving in extreme slow motion, as if you are doing Tai Chi. Pretend you are an astronaut floating weightlessly in space. Relax and allow gravity to flow down through your body, releasing tension. Relax and allow your tensions to melt away.

Your mind should be calm. But do not try to will yourself to be calm, which could create further anxiety and tension. Let go. Although you strive to eschew wandering thoughts, should any extraneous thoughts intrude, do not resist them, or scold yourself for not concentrating. Simply do not attach to them; observe them flitting by and then return to focusing on rhythmic breathing. Gradually your mind will become tranquil, just as rhythmic rocking eventually soothes a baby.

Qi Gong

A specialized form of ancient Chinese energy-cultivating exercises for healing, promoting longevity, and protection against illness is called Qi Gong. Although Qi Gong is one of China's cultural treasures, developed by Taoist and Buddhist adepts centuries ago, the benefits of these simple yet profound exercises have only recently been discovered and appreciated in the West.

What is particularly valuable about these exercises, once jealously guarded secrets, is that they can be performed by the elderly and those who are ill or bedridden, since there is a minimum amount of muscular exertion. Yet the health benefits are often extraordinary, and recent scientific studies seem to corroborate traditional claims that Qi Gong can actually alleviate some chronic diseases and promote longevity.

The Universal Form can be also done as a Qi Gong exercise. By holding each of the five hand positions, visualizing and using our will to direct the internal *qi,* or energy flow, we are able to transform the Universal Form into a potent Qi Gong exercise.

However, the profound medical and philosophical theory underlying Qi Gong exceeds the scope of this present book, which is to introduce the Universal Form primarily as a simple stress-reducing exercise. Practicing the Universal Form for Qi Gong or energy training may be the subject of a future book.

Daily Practice

Just as you would not wait until you had a cavity before brushing your teeth, so too should you not wait until stress cripples you to begin practicing the Universal Form. Remember: practice daily even when you don't feel stressed. Consistent practice is preventive medicine that fosters health.

In the beginning, it is common to have difficulty practicing. Although we may acknowledge the benefits, it is difficult to get motivated. Too often, the initial enthusiasm, a burst of devoted practice for the first week or even several months, wanes. Your goal is to go the distance. The Universal Form, along with the concepts of Tri-Harmony, can enhance your physical and mental well-being your whole life long. For this reason, take it easy at first. Begin with a gentle discipline. Don't bully yourself into practicing. Otherwise, sooner or later, you will rebel and stop practicing altogether.

Do not think of the form as a boring discipline that you must do. Do not be a spiritual drill sergeant. Many students who initially resist practice begin to enjoy the Universal Form after they change their attitude about doing it. Have fun. Play with it. Don't be rigid. Listen to music while practicing.

Schedule Practice into Your Daily Routine

Practice is prayer!

The Tri-Harmony Universal Form should become part of your life. Consistent practice over time will develop into an unshakable habit. By scheduling this into your life and making it part of your lifestyle, like washing your face in the morning, you will train yourself to center daily. Centering will become a habit that is incorporated into your daily routine, and something you won't want to live without.

An excellent time to practice the Universal Form is first thing in the morning. Many of us begin our day jolted out of sleep by an alarm, then stagger out of bed, wash, gulp down a cup of coffee and dash off to the office, beginning and continuing the day unbalanced and harried. Instead, you can begin the day centered: calm, focused, and with a sense of well-being that will carry you through the day. By doing three Universal Forms before you dash off, you also will find that you are more efficient and alert. At night, a gentle meditative Universal Form can help you wind down from the day and fall asleep with ease.

The Universal Form can be used in other ways as well. A business person can slip into the wash room and practice a Universal Form before engaging in a tough business negotiation. If you cannot find a private space to practice, simply close you eyes where you are and visualize doing the form accompanied by deep breathing. This can help you feel calm and alert even in the most intense business situations.

A famous rock musician uses the Universal Form in the recording studio during grueling all-night sessions. When tempers flare and the atmosphere turns tense, he will go into another room, shut the door and practice the Universal Form to revitalize himself. A concert pianist practices a Universal Form to calm and center himself in preparation for his performance. Likewise, investment bankers, advertising executives, Olympic athletes, artists and children have all found the Universal Form highly beneficial.

Mastering the Universal Form

The Universal Form has many levels. Since the sequence can be learned within one to three classes, students often assume they have mastered it after practicing it routinely for a few months. Like many martial art forms, however, there are layers of hidden meaning to the form, but they must be sought out. They are not easily revealed. Higher knowledge is always subtle. Often what is not apparent to the student is evident to those with deeper understanding acquired over time.

A common mistake many students make is to fall into the trap of routinely performing the Universal Form without variation. Although such students may be perfect technically and achieve the benefits that particular variation offers, they have limited the depth of their understanding of the form.

Habits are mechanical behavior, representing the antithesis of the goal of the Universal Form, which strives for awareness of movement. Avoid practicing the form as an empty ritual devoid of meaning. Practice with spirit. The form must become alive as you use it, a vehicle for self-expression. Continually explore the different ways of doing the form. Allow your body's awareness and its intelligence to experience the different variations of the form. Although you may enjoy the strenuous muscle conditioning method, try alternating it with the aerobic method. Or if you are inclined toward the more gentle stretching method, try alternating it with muscle toning. Expanding your consciousness of your body will enable you to develop new ways of moving. Aim for versatility.

At different stages of life, you may tend to prefer one method over another. Usually young adults prefer the dynamic-tension method and as we get older we soften up and gravitate to stretching and meditation. Our preference for one method over another reflects our personal empowerment.

Mastery of the form is achieved when the movements become natural and spontaneous. You are no longer bound by a way and a form, but you can playfully experiment with different variations depending on how your body feels at the moment. But no matter how you do it, you will benefit as long as when you do it, you give it your best.

Ultimately, each variation of the form is but a different means of centering. In the early stages of learning the form, simply doing it is enough. But as you mature, you want to begin to feel it. As you master the movements, you will begin to live it.

On the edge—
Transforming Stress
to Power

Chapter 5

Application in Daily Life

The Universal Form is an excellent centering method for controlling stress. However, there are times when we may need to center but it may not be convenient to do the form. What can we do if we want to de-stress immediately? How can we center?

This problem is solved by using Tri-Harmony centering techniques derived from the Universal Form. These techniques offer the benefits of the Universal Form but they can be practiced less conspicuously, if the time or the place is inappropriate to practice the form. They are practical and they work.

Stress is related to our state of being, how we feel either mentally or physically. Our mind, emotional equilibrium, attitude, and energy level influence how we deal with stressful situations. An unpleasant encounter with another person, though stress inducing, can have positive or negative results depending upon how we respond.

Changing Our State of Being to Control Stress

A common folk remedy for coping with anger is to hold the breath and count to ten; another is to take ten deep breaths. Although these methods may be regarded simply as old superstitions, they nevertheless have some scientific basis. Apparently there is a relationship between breathing and emotions.

Moreover, there are characteristic traits, "body language," that expresses the way we feel physically or psychologically. For example, when angry our muscles tighten. Our breathing pattern is different when we are happy than when we are unhappy. We stand differently when we are alert than when we are fatigued. Obviously, there is a correlation between our state of being—our emotional state and energy level—and our posture, physiology, and muscles. When we are stressed, even if the cause of stress cannot be identified or immediately resolved, we can still reduce stress by consciously changing these elements. The key to decreasing muscular tension, alleviating anxiety, and energizing is thus to be found in altering our movement, concentration, and breathing.

The Universal Form, as we have seen, relates to the following scientific disciplines:

1. Biomechanics, the principles of physics applied to human movement
2. Psychology, especially the effects of concentration, mental awareness, and emotional calm on behavior
3. Physiology, the function of our bodies' internal processes and how they affect emotions, feelings, and behavior.

Reading the Body

Before we can effectively employ biomechanical, psychological, and physiological centering techniques, we must cultivate an acute awareness of our moods, feelings, and body. Unless we first detect the signs of stress, we will not know when to use the techniques. Unfortunately, we have become so accustomed to stressful living that we often don't even know we are stressed until it is too late. Therefore it is important to learn to identify stress symptoms through self-awareness.

Centering is subtle. It requires an awareness of the two extremes of psychological equilibrium and physical equilibrium, as well as an acute sensitivity to their ever-changing relationship. Psychologically, our mood swings directly affect our stress levels. Physically, our appetite, fatigue, and degree of fitness on a particular day are considerations that influence our stress levels and behavior.

Learn to read your body, to listen and feel the non-verbal messages of your physical being. Learn to detect the common symptoms of stress: ailments such as headaches, lower backache, or tension in the neck and shoulders. In addition to noticing physical symptoms, you should also observe emotional symptoms of stress: depression, irritability, negativity, and overall sour moods.

Each person's body has a unique way of signaling that something is wrong. For some it is a sore throat, for others it is dizziness, or perhaps the swelling of an old injury. Recognizing our personal warning signs, early indicators that our immune system is vulnerable is a valuable way to know when to practice our centering techniques. Common physical symptoms include headache, backache, digestive disorders, skin rashes, and painfully tensed muscles. The psychological symptoms associated with stress include chronic anger, depression, anxiety and a feeling of helplessness. Observe your body's own idiosyncrasies. Discover your individual warning signals, they tell you when your system is overly stressed.

Beside the relationship of physical and mental factors in maintaining healthful equilibrium, it is necessary to realize the equally crucial relationship our being has with the external world: the weather, personal, and professional relationships, family, the economic and political situation, ecological awareness are all intricately connected with our sense of well-being. Many of these external factors that we cannot control. This being the case, we must condition ourselves not to become distraught over them.

Regular practice of the Universal Form will gradually culti-vate a heightened kino-esthetic sense within us. This sensitivi-ty to our bodily functions is normally taken for granted. By reading your body, you are consciously monitoring yourself to detect the symptoms of stress. By learning to feel and under-stand the subtle changes in your physical, mental, and emo-tional states you can detect the tension before more serious symptoms erupt. Then you can take the appropriate measures to reduce stress.

Another common problem is thinking that we are too busy to de-stress. Don't wait. Your efficiency is enhanced when you are centered. New awareness and persistence in breaking old behavioral patterns and replacing them with new habits are critical in order to use any centering technique. Begin by rec-ognizing stress and then allow yourself to stop and practice a centering technique. By immediately stopping what you are doing, no matter how important, to do a minute of centering exercises, you will change your state of being. You will discov-er the advantages: greater vitality, mental clarity, and sense of wellness. With centering techniques we can create radical change in our behavior, attitude, and emotions by changing our posture, muscular tension, and breathing pattern.

The Golden Cord Technique

According to the principle of Tri-Harmony, a human being stands between heaven and earth, possessing energies from both the spiritual and material realms. Perhaps by imagining a large tree, but a tree with consciousness, will make this concept more vivid. Think of the tree with its roots going deep beneath the earth, getting nourishing chemicals and water from the soil, while at the same time getting carbon dioxide and the energy of sunlight through its branches and leaves. This is lit-erally receiving the energies of heaven and earth.

Balancing the opposites as a means to harmony is reflected on the physical level in how we stand. For the simple act of standing erect can be considered a physical metaphor for the philosophical notion of the Tri-Harmony. Neither the idealistic

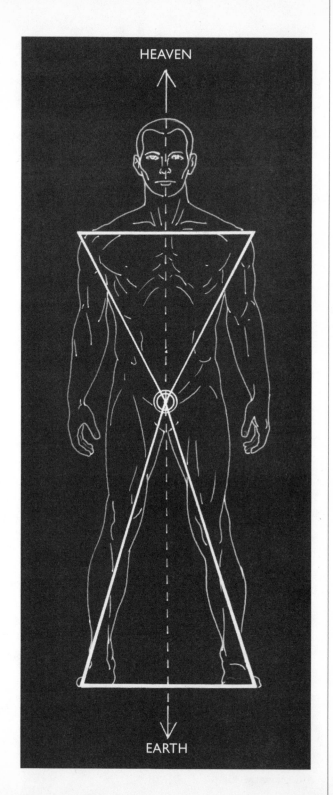

THE GOLDEN CORD TECHNIQUE allows us to realign ourselves quickly to draw energy from heaven, while releasing tension into the earth.

dreamer with his or her head in the clouds, unable to handle worldly affairs, nor the pragmatic realist with feet planted in the material world yet incapable of aspiring to lofty visions, is to be emulated. The enlightened human must responsibly balance the forces of heaven and earth in order to create harmony.

Philosophically, to cling to any extreme— whether excessive idealism (heaven) or pragmatism (earth), excessive spiritual asceticism (heaven), or sensual hedonism (earth)—creates a distorted view of reality. On the physical level, to extend our spine upward into space, to "will" ourselves heavenward, without being grounded and rooted to the earth, or, on the other hand, to be rooted by the earth's force of gravity, without extending our spine upward, creates postural imbalance that directly and negatively influences our state of mind.

A person who is depressed usually has drooping shoulders and slumps. In contrast, a person with too much energy is hyper-tense, agitated, and nervous. The healthy person manages to balance these opposite extremes; an energetic and enthusiastic person's posture is relatively upright. The shoulders are up, but relaxed not tense; and the back is straight, naturally curved, not stiff.

The key to standing correctly is the "golden cord," an imaginary rope or string connected to the top of our heads that stretches our spine straight upward as if pulling us up to heaven. When you feel tired, depressed, or enervated, you can temporarily change your mental state simply by standing or sitting up straight. Pull yourself up with your golden cord, back straight, chin tucked in, shoulders back, and breathing deeply. This is like snapping to attention in the military but with a major difference—you are relaxed. Except for your erect spine, all the muscles of your body are relaxed. By changing your posture, you are sending neurological signals through your body to be alert, vital, and resourceful.

To practice the golden cord technique, just snap to attention as if you are a puppet suddenly pulled up by a cord attached to your head. Draw yourself up by straightening your back. Bring your shoulders up in a shrugging motion, then draw them back by squeezing your shoulder blades together, as you inhale deeply. Inhale through your nose and feel your lungs becoming filled with air. Hold your breath for three seconds as you concentrate on tensing your neck and the muscles of your upper back. Then slowly relax. Allow your shoulders to return to a normal upright position as you exhale. When exhaling, open your mouth and let out a heavy sighing sound.

Remember, we cannot force ourselves to relax. Relaxation is simply to let go. Allow the force of gravity to naturally pull on your body and limbs, and to draw the tension out of the muscles. Feel tension melt away as it flows down into the earth.

Concentration is crucial. Attention must be focused on concentrating your muscles when you draw yourself up. This creates an upward tension that straightens your spine and realigns your skeletal structure in a balanced and symmetrical position. When releasing, except for the minimum effort required to pull up your golden cord, the muscles of your body are completely relaxed. Relax by letting go.

Breathing must be synchronized with the alternating pull-upward-release-downward movements. Inhale when your "golden cord pulls upward to heaven," straighten your spine, and contract your muscles. Exhale when you "root yourself to earth," relax your muscles, and allow gravity to drain any excess tension from your body. Mentally focus on the quality of each breath. Consciously feel yourself breathe and smell the air as it is drawn into your lungs. Repeat this three times, to reinforce your body's feel for correct postural alignment. Do this often and as an exercise, until it becomes a conditioned response. Make it a daily habit to realign your spine several times a day.

In summary, the "golden cord technique" balances contraction, the conscious straightening of the spine, and relaxation, the releasing of the muscles. This is a practical manifestation of the Tri-Harmony principle, where the human force balances the forces of heaven and earth.

The Shoulder Roll Technique

Did you know that it is impossible to be angry if your body is totally relaxed? When we are in a positive or negative mood our bodies unconsciously reflect our inner state. Study an angry person and you will notice that the facial muscles tighten, especially around the jaws and mouth. Similarly when we are upset or uptight our shoulders rise and our muscles in our back and neck tighten. On the other hand, if a person is depressed and sad, the head and shoulders droop.

Since there are physiological responses to anger and stress, instead of trying to control stressful emotions through rational commands to yourself, which may only aggravate you even more, try instead to control your body. Try just relaxing and dropping your shoulders. You will be changing the messages to your nervous system and the brain.

A high degree of control over all muscle groups is developed after prolonged practice of the Universal Form. This heightened kino-esthetic awareness is useful for consciously relaxing our tensed-up neck and shoulder muscles when we need to relieve tension accumulated from the pressures of office or home. By practicing the Shoulder Roll Technique for a few minutes, we can stretch our limbs, circulate our blood, combat mental fatigue and refresh ourselves. This technique can be done standing or sitting.

Draw your shoulders up and drop your head back so the back of your head presses against your upper back. Close your eyes tightly. At the same time, clench both your hands into tight fists. You are contracting the already over-tensed muscles of your neck and shoulders and bringing the muscular tension to the maximum level. As you scrunch up your neck inhale slowly, deliberately, and deeply through your nose. Fill your lungs to maximum capacity. Hold your breath for three seconds, then suddenly relax your muscles by dropping your shoulders, opening your hands, and return your head to its regular position.

Coordinate these motions with a sharp prolonged exhalation through your mouth. Make a sound as if you are sighing. This removes the toxins from your body. Repeat this two more times. For the second and third repetitions, your exhalation should be longer and smoother. The louder and more drawn out the better.

After this, immediately follow up with circular neck rotations. Drop your head forward while relaxing completely.

Allow gravity to pull down on your head. Don't use muscular force. Slowly rotate your head around. Inhale smoothly and deeply for the first half of the circle and exhale smoothly and deeply on the second half of the rotation, as you return your head to the starting position. Turn your head clockwise about three times and then three turns counterclockwise. Again, coordinate your breathing with the movements and be sure to make a deep, sighing sound. Your movements should be slow, smooth, and rhythmic.

Three repetitions of shoulder crunches followed by six neck rotations in each direction will loosen the stiff muscles in your shoulders, neck and head, increase circulation into these areas, and send fresh oxygen into the brain. You will immediately feel soothed and invigorated.

Breathing Techniques

Healthy breathing is important for healthy living. Yet many people today do not breath correctly. Since breathing is a natural, instinctive function, this may sound ludicrous. Unfortunately, we have lost touch with our instinctive rhythms as we adapt ourselves to the artificial rhythms of a technological lifestyle.

Take six to ten deep breaths. On the last inhalation close your eyes and hold your breath. Feel your self energize. Feel the oxygen circulating through your body. Hold your breath until it is almost uncomfortable, but do not strain. After a few seconds slowly exhale through your mouth. Allow your normal breathing pattern to return while concentrating on relaxing the muscles of your body. Then open your eyes and feel energized.

The Seashore Breathing Technique

Retreating to the seashore and listening to the pounding surf has been universally regarded as a source of solace, inspiration, and personal healing. Perhaps the sound of the tide evokes our earliest memories as infants engulfed by the rhythms of breathing or heartbeats echoing in our mother's womb. In any case, when our lives become harried and overwhelming we often wish we could escape to a quiet beach.

One centering technique that combines breathing and mental visualization can bring us on an ocean holiday. Sit comfortably or lie down. Close your eyes, relax, and inhale deeply through your nose. Your breathing cycle should imitate the sound of the surf. With practice, the gentle inhalation through your nose will sound like the waves rolling out to sea and the more powerful sound of your exhaling will seem like the tide washing to shore. To further help you mentally re-create a realistic ocean roar, open your mouth so the rear of your throat acts as an echo chamber when you expel air. Relax and listen intently to the waves rhythmically crashing to shore and drawing out to sea. At the same time, visualize being on a deserted beach under white clouds and blue sky. Feel the warm sun on your skin as you relax and lie on the sand. Smell the crisp salt air. Use your imagination.

The combination of the inner visual image, audio cue, and imagined sensations will stimulate a seashore environment. Your body and nervous system will be relaxed and soothed. As you develop the ability to visualize and imagine, you can perfect the sound of the ebb tide and you will be able to instantly find refuge on your own private beach. So whenever you want to stop the world and get off, close your eyes and practice the Seashore Breathing Technique.

Deep Breathing for Energizing

Healthy breathing requires us to breathe from our diaphragm. Inhalation causes the diaphragm to descend and push gently against the abdomen. Exhalation causes the diaphragm to ascend, and push the abdominal wall inward. When practicing, concentrate on breathing deeply from the lower abdomen. Place your hands on your lower belly, beneath your navel. You should feel your abdomen moving in and out, drawing the oxygen deep into the lungs for greater circulation throughout the body.

By breathing deeply and forcefully as we do when practicing the Universal Form body-conditioning method, we can provide ourselves with a sudden burst of energy and vitality. Such an ability was obviously valued by warriors who needed to re-energize in the midst of arduous fighting. For us today, this ability is useful when we are driving long distances or working late at the office.

Again start from a centered posture, feet shoulder-width apart. You can sit or stand. (It is best to sit, until you learn the proper inhalation and exhalation rhythm, since it is possible to become dizzy when first learning.) Align your spine by using your imaginary golden cord. Inhale deeply through your nose as you expand your lower belly, not your chest, to full capacity. Pause a beat, then release. Open your mouth and exhale sharply yet smoothly. Make a loud sighing sound. Continue to exhale even after you think you've fully exhaled. Your exhalation will be longer than your inhalation. Pause a beat, then begin again. Continue this deep breathing while concentrating on the flow of air and the rhythmic inhaling and exhaling.

Begin carefully to prevent dizziness. Start off gently, without straining, and don't hyperventilate. It is essential to become aware of balancing your oxygen intake with the expulsion of carbon dioxide. After you master this inhalation and exhalation cycle, you will be able to control the air volume so you will not become dizzy from taking in too little or too much oxygen.

Remember: Inhale through your nose, slowly and deeply, and exhale through your mouth, smoothly and sharply. As with all breathing, be aware of the quality of the breath: the sound, the texture, the quantity of air, the depth, the flow, the smoothness, and the refinement.

In the flow of existence,

I have seen many forms,
   I have done many forms,
      I have been many forms,

Each form holding a key to another gate of reality.

When I saw the Universal Form
   I saw the dance of stillness.

When I did the Universal Form,
   I felt like a tree on a mountain top.

When I do the Universal Form
   Heaven and Earth become one
         and
   I am the key to the gates of eternity.

—Gil Yedidia

Chapter 6

Afterword

The supreme goal of Shaolin martial arts training is inner harmony. Thus for the warrior monk the zenith of fighting ability is epitomized, paradoxically, in never having to fight. Ideally, the true master has cultivated the sensitivity to avoid a life-threatening situation in the first place. Such a solution to self-defense, so simple and yet so profound, requires an ultra-heightened awareness accompanied by the capacity for decisive action. So, too, should we have in matters concerning health, according to the Tri-Harmony philosophy.

The Tri-Harmony teaching is not so much a specific technique, exercise, or method but rather a holistic learning model, an attitude, and a practical approach to healthy living for those committed to taking responsibility for their place in the scheme of things. For in the end, our health and happiness rests not with others or the world outside us, but within ourselves. Each of us alone must realize this universal wisdom and then we can take appropriate action for our own well-being. To do so we must cultivate self-awareness to detect early stress symptoms and then practice self-care techniques to prevent them from developing into illness.

TRI-HARMONY PRINCIPLES
are reflected in the
steps through which
they are applied to life.
We must know them,
do them, and feel
them before we can
truly live them.

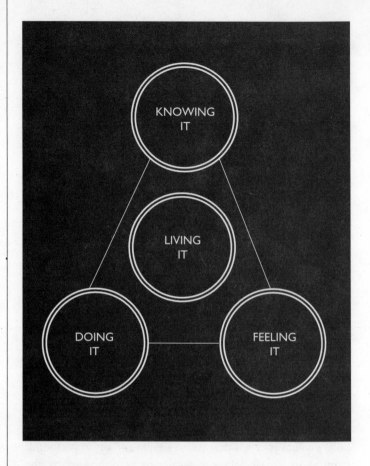

Knowing it is it. But knowledge alone is not enough; it must be transformed into action. Unless we re-educate ourselves to take a new attitude toward health and create healthier habits of living, the information itself is useless.

Doing it is it. It is one thing to know what to do, but we must, more importantly, do what we know. Action is the completion of knowledge. Daily practice of the Universal Form and application of centering techniques when necessary throughout the day, will gradually become a habit.

Feeling it is it. Practicing a dull routine mechanically like an empty ritual is almost as bad as not doing it. Students can be sure they have made progress when they can feel the exercise.

At this stage, the form becomes alive and it becomes an expression of the individual.

Living it is it. We must internalize the habit of Tri-Harmony centering. Once the attitude of health and the physical principles become part of you, and once you become adept and sensitive to the mind, body relationship, de-stressing will become a natural and spontaneous activity. There is nothing to think about. Just as when irritated your body unconsciously triggers you to sneeze, when overly stressed you will automatically respond by centering. You can either relax or energize through mind, muscle, and breath control.

In order to promote health and combat stress, the Universal Form is a valuable aid for surviving, striving, and thriving in our hectic contemporary world. This modern moving meditation exercise, based on traditional Shaolin martial arts and Zen principles, is a way for us to transform stress to power and inner peace.

About the Author

Lawrence Tan holds a B.A. in comparative religion from Boston University and is a Shaolin Kung Fu master. He has taught both traditional martial arts and his own self-care therapy of Tri-Harmony for over thirty years, both at his own studio and through lectures and workshops at institutions such as the C.G. Jung Foundation and New York Medical College. His students range from corporate executives, doctors, lawyers, and Olympic athletes to media personalities such as Lou Reed and Billy Idol. A video presentation of the Universal Form, titled *Three Minutes to Power and Peace,* received the 1997 Silver Apple Award from the National Education Media Network, and is available from Wellspring Media (1-800-538-5856). An animated version of the Universal Form is also available on the internet, at www.triharmony.com

The author and his son Tatanka.

The "weathermark" identifies this book as a production of Weatherhill, Inc., publishers of fine books on Asia and the Pacific. Editorial supervision: Ray Furse. Book and cover design: Mariana Canelo. Production supervision: Bill Rose. Printing and binding: R.R. Donnelley & Sons. The typefaces used are Garamond and Gill Sans.